POPULARITY

A Bridge between Classical and Behavioral Finance

Roger G. Ibbotson, Thomas M. Idzorek, CFA,
Paul D. Kaplan, CFA, and James X. Xiong, CFA

CFA Institute
Research
Foundation

Statement of Purpose

The CFA Institute Research Foundation is a not-for-profit organization established to promote the development and dissemination of relevant research for investment practitioners worldwide.

CFA®, Chartered Financial Analyst®, and GIPS® are just a few of the trademarks owned by CFA Institute. To view a list of CFA Institute trademarks and the Guide for the Use of CFA Institute Marks, please visit our website at www.cfainstitute.org.

This publication is designed to provide accurate and authoritative information in regard to the subject matter covered. It is sold with the understanding that the publisher is not engaged in rendering legal, accounting, or other professional service. If legal advice or other expert assistance is required, the services of a competent professional should be sought.

Cover photo credit: Ho Ngoc Binh / Moment / Getty Images

ISBN 978-1-944960-60-5

Biographies

Roger G. Ibbotson is Professor in the Practice Emeritus of Finance at Yale School of Management. He is also chairman of Zebra Capital Management, LLC, a global equity investment and hedge fund manager. Professor Ibbotson is founder and former chairman of Ibbotson Associates, now a Morningstar company. He has written numerous books and articles, including "Stocks, Bonds, Bills, and Inflation" with Rex Sinquefield (updated annually), which serves as a standard reference for information and capital market returns. Professor Ibbotson conducts research on a broad range of financial topics, including popularity, liquidity, investment returns, mutual funds, international markets, portfolio management, and valuation. He recently published *The Equity Risk Premium* and *Lifetime Financial Advice*. Professor Ibbotson has also co-authored two books with Gary Brinson, *Global Investing* and *Investment Markets*. He is a regular contributor to and editorial board member of both trade and academic journals and serves on numerous boards, including Dimensional Fund Advisors' funds. Professor Ibbotson frequently speaks at universities, conferences, and other forums. He received his bachelor's degree in mathematics from Purdue University, his MBA from Indiana University, and his PhD from the University of Chicago, where he taught for more than 10 years and served as executive director of CRSP.

Thomas M. Idzorek, CFA, is chief investment officer, retirement, for Morningstar Investment Management LLC. He also serves as a member of Morningstar's 401(k) committee and Public Policy Council, chair of Morningstar's overall Research Council, and as a member on the editorial boards of *Morningstar* magazine and the CFA Institute *Financial Analysts Journal*. Idzorek was formerly president of Morningstar's global investment management division, where he oversaw the firm's global investment advice, consulting, retirement solutions, broker/dealer, index, and financial wellness businesses. Additionally, he has served as president of Ibbotson Associates, president of Morningstar Associates, board member/responsible officer for a number of Morningstar Investment Management subsidiaries, global chief investment officer for Morningstar Investment Management, chief investment officer for Ibbotson Associates, and director of research and product development for Ibbotson. Most recently, Idzorek served as head of investment methodology and economic research for Morningstar. Before joining Ibbotson, he was a senior quantitative researcher for Zephyr Associates.

Idzorek has written numerous articles for academic and industry journals and collaborated on papers that have won a *Financial Analysts Journal* Graham & Dodd Scroll Award. He is an expert on multiasset class strategic asset allocation, the Black–Litterman model, target date funds, retirement income solutions, fund-of-funds optimization, risk budgeting, and performance analysis. Idzorek is the key methodological creator of Morningstar's target date and retirement managed account (robo-advice) solution. He holds a bachelor's degree in marketing from Arizona State University and a master's degree in business administration from Thunderbird School of Global Management.

Paul D. Kaplan, CFA, is director of research for Morningstar Canada and is a senior member of Morningstar's global research team. He led the development of many of the quantitative methodologies behind Morningstar's fund analysis, indexes, adviser tools, and other services. Kaplan conducts research on asset allocation, retirement income planning, portfolio construction, index methodologies, and other investment topics. Many of his research papers have been published in professional books and publications, such as the *Financial Analysts Journal* and the *Journal of Portfolio Management*, and he has served on the editorial board of the *Financial Analysts Journal*. Kaplan has received a Graham & Dodd Top Award and a Graham & Dodd Award of Excellence. Many of his works appear in his book *Frontiers of Modern Asset Allocation*. Previously, he has served as quantitative research director for Morningstar Europe in London, director of quantitative research in the United States, and chief investment officer of Morningstar Associates, LLC, where he developed and managed the investment methodology for Morningstar's retirement planning and advice services. Previously, Kaplan was a vice president of Ibbotson Associates and served as the firm's chief economist and director of research. Prior to that, he served on the economics faculty of Northwestern University, where he taught international finance and statistics. Kaplan holds a bachelor's degree in mathematics, economics, and computer science from New York University and a master's degree and doctorate in economics from Northwestern University.

James X. Xiong, CFA, is head of scientific investment management research at Morningstar Investment Management. He leads research and develops new methodologies and algorithms on the time-varying capital markets model, tail risk management, portfolio optimization, asset allocation, dynamic portfolio choice, insurance product allocation, mutual fund selection, alternative asset class investments, Monte Carlo simulations, and other investment and financial planning areas. Xiong's work has been published in the *Financial Analysts Journal, Journal of Investment Management, Journal of Portfolio Management, Journal of Risk Management in Financial Institutions,* and *Journal of Financial Planning,* among other publications. His co-authored "Liquidity Style of Mutual Funds" was awarded with a Graham & Dodd Scroll, and his co-authored "Momentum, Acceleration and Reversal" won a Harry M. Markowitz Award. Xiong has published more than 15 papers in scientific journals, including *Physical Review Letters,* a prestigious world journal in physics. He holds a bachelor's degree in physics from Wuhan University in China and a doctorate in physics from the University of Houston.

Contents

This publication qualifies for 4.5 CE credits under the guidelines of the CFA Institute Continuing Education Program.

Foreword

Why does value investing work? Why do other factor strategies work? For that matter, why does *any* active strategy—meaning, any strategy other than capitalization-weighted indexing—"work" in the sense of having a reasonable chance of beating the cap-weighted index other than by random variation? The answer could lie in classical finance, or behavioral finance, or both.

The Classical Answer

Classical finance posits that all investors are rational and fully informed. This starting point seems to lead to a recommendation to index all assets, but that advice is not necessarily where it leads.

Although most of classical finance focuses only on risk and expected return, investors differ in their tastes and preferences and assets differ in their characteristics other than risk and expected return. These observations, which form the basis for the current book, are the essence of an article that predates this book, written way back in 1984, by Roger Ibbotson, Jeffrey Diermeier (then, at Brinson Partners, and now, the Diermeier Family Foundation), and myself. The article, entitled "The Demand for Capital Market Returns: A New Equilibrium Theory," incorporates investor preferences—sometimes called "clientele effects"—into an equilibrium framework conforming to neo-classical economics and classical finance. The connection between the more recent popularity framework and the new equilibrium framework from 1984 was made in an unpublished manuscript started by Tom Idzorek that has evolved into this book. The new equilibrium framework is based on the assertion that economic agents are rational utility maximizers. Classical finance does not say what information agents should *not* look at, as long as they behave rationally.

For example, one investor could be strongly averse to illiquidity whereas another is not, or one investor might pay taxes at a different rate than another. Everybody's different. Moreover, we differ in more than simply risk aversion, so we are motivated to hold substantively different portfolios, not just index funds levered up or down to the desired risk level. I will revisit these ideas in greater detail when I discuss how our 1984 effort links with the current book. But for now, I want to note that just observing differences among investors doesn't mean you can beat the market. Let's add in the fact that some of the investor groups that like or dislike an attribute common to a group of assets are numerous and control a lot of money. If a large, well-funded group of people avoids (or pays less for) an asset because it has an attribute they don't like, that asset might be attractively priced from the viewpoint of an investor who doesn't care about that attribute. An active manager might buy that asset.

A portfolio of assets accumulated according to this rule should beat the market (on average over time). This clientele effect is consistent with classical finance, broadly understood, and the possibility of adding alpha within a classical finance paradigm.

The Behavioral Answer

Active investment strategies could also work for *behavioral* reasons, in the sense of allowing for the possibility (I'd call it a fact) that not all investor preferences are rational or well-informed. Researchers have accumulated a great deal of evidence that investors are *not* fully rational and are *far from* fully informed. They do all kinds of crazy stuff. It seems like it ought to be profitable to take advantage of that fact.

Reducing the Complexity of the Market

Whichever story you subscribe to, classical or behavioral—and both could apply—the market is very complex. It contains far more securities than can be practical to analyze individually. To reduce the units of analysis to a manageable number, researchers and investment managers have compressed securities and their attributes into *factors*, such as value, momentum, liquidity, and profitability. This technique is well-known, so I will not describe it here.

The number of factors observable in the markets is still considerable, but the number is far higher than logic suggests should exist. So, a valuable contribution would be to identify a common theme that links the factors in a way that makes economic sense and is consistent with the clientele-driven equilibrium described in the 1984 paper. That link is one of the aspirations of this new CFA Institute Research Foundation book by my former business associates and friends, Roger Ibbotson and Paul Kaplan, and their current colleagues, Thomas Idzorek and James Xiong (hereafter, IIKX).

The phenomenon that IIKX have identified as explaining a great deal about the cross-section of equity returns is *popularity* or, to stand the issue on its head and consider what explains *excess* returns, *unpopularity*. Specifically, any characteristic that drives away investors in sufficient number—for whatever reason—and causes the demand curve for an investment to shift to the left (meaning less demand) is a characteristic you should seek out.

Popularity is not, itself, a factor. It is a framework for understanding and predicting factors.

How Popularity and Other Factors Set Prices

This book incorporates the popularity framework into an equilibrium setting, meaning that the quantity of each asset supplied equals the quantity demanded and all assets are voluntarily held by somebody. Such an equilibrium can apply under the assumptions of either classical or behavioral finance.

As long as aggregate preferences are relatively stable over time, they will play a role in setting asset prices. The preferences can be rational (classical), irrational (behavioral), or a combination of the two. The investors with weaker aversion to generally disliked characteristics will load up on the less popular stocks, which will have higher expected returns. Those with stronger aversion to those characteristics will willingly accept lower expected returns. Because the equilibrium includes all preferences, the popularity framework provides a "bridge" between classical and behavioral finance.

Want to learn more? Read the book, especially Chapter 4, which summarizes the 1984 article. Like Johnny Appleseed, our article scattered the seeds that would grow into various bushes and plants in subsequent decades and, finally, into the tree that is this book.

From New Equilibrium Theory to the Popularity Asset Pricing Model

We called our proposition NET, New Equilibrium Theory, partly because it examined returns *net* of all the additions and subtractions for desired and undesired characteristics (Ibbotson, Diermeier, and Siegel 1984). At the time, a wag (sounds better than a critic) remarked that as Voltaire said about the Holy Roman Empire—it was neither holy, nor Roman, nor an empire—our NET was neither new, nor equilibrium, nor a theory.

Of course, the wag was mostly correct. NET was just an application of the principles of Economics 101 to finance, so it was not new in any of its elemental parts, although the assembly was new. The equilibrium it described is not fully general. And although NET meets the philosophical definition of a theory—an integrated body of knowledge that explains a wide variety of phenomena—it did not have the full mathematical development that it deserved until the current book.

Having been crafted into proper form in Chapter 5 of this book as the popularity asset pricing model (PAPM), NET now *is* a fully mathematized theory. Combining elements of both classical and behavioral finance, the PAPM follows the rich traditions of neoclassical microeconomics. Specifically, it is based on the following pillars of economic theory as applied to finance:

- *Subjectivism*—The values of assets are not determined solely by their inherent properties. Investor preferences play a major role in determining value.

- *Marginalism*—Each investor constructs his or her portfolio so that the marginal contribution to utility of each asset is equal to the marginal cost of holding the asset—namely, its price.

- *Equilibrium*—Asset prices are determined in markets so that all assets are willingly held.

Understanding Historical Returns

The authors of this book, along with various collaborators of theirs, have gathered quite a few of the pieces of modern finance—pieces that, when assembled, begin to explain a lot about the way assets are priced and portfolios are constructed. Let's start at the beginning: "Stocks, Bonds, Bills, and Inflation: Year-by-Year Historical Returns (1926–1974)" by Roger Ibbotson and Rex Sinquefield (1976a).

This familiar work, originally published in the University of Chicago's *Journal of Business* in 1976, was released as a book by the CFA Institute Research Foundation in 1977 (when the organization was called the Financial Analysts Federation). The book achieved wide distribution and influence. It addresses one of the components of NET theory: risk. How much risk is in each asset class, and what is the market price of each risk? That is, how much compensation in the form of higher return do investors, as a group, require for taking a given amount of risk?

Ibbotson and Sinquefield answered the questions of risk by measuring how much investors *got* as compensation for the various risks in the market. Asserting that investors conform their expectation of reward-for-risk to that which proves achievable in the market, the authors concluded that the realized reward—which, the authors revealed, had been quite large for equities as compared with bonds and bills—was a satisfactory indicator of the expected or required reward.

A New Kind of Forecasting

This insight opened up a new avenue for forecasting. Ibbotson and Sinquefield (1976b) not only measured the average return on each asset class, and thus on the difference between asset classes; they also documented all of the monthly and annual returns. Doing so made it possible to measure the variability of returns—that is, the *amount of risk* for which investors were being rewarded—not just the size of the reward.

By "pricing" risk in this way, Ibbotson and Sinquefield were able to extrapolate past returns into the future (making an adjustment for interest rates). They not only estimated the mean or expected return on each asset class; they also forecast the *whole distribution* of potential future returns. They called these extrapolations "probabilistic forecasts."

People were already familiar with probabilistic forecasts of the weather, but in investment finance they were something new and different. Under Ibbotson and Sinquefield's influence, probabilistic forecasts have become standard practice in financial planning.[1] "You have an X% chance of earning at least Y%"—a phrase that would have baffled most planners before Ibbotson and Sinquefield did their pioneering work—is now heard everywhere. The emphasis on risk, on deviation from the expectation, is the most important benefit of this approach.

The Supply of Capital Market Returns

But where did the money come from to provide these rich rewards?

In a companion paper to "The Demand for Capital Market Returns," Diermeier, Ibbotson, and I noted that the aggregate return to investors in the capital markets must be set by the amount of profit that corporations can earn in the real economy.[2] We called our paper "The Supply of Capital Market Returns" (Diermeier, Ibbotson, and Siegel 1984), where we observed that corporate profits cannot grow indefinitely (and are unlikely to shrink indefinitely) as a percentage of GDP; thus, real corporate profit growth should proceed at about the rate of real GDP growth over the very long run.

Price-to-earnings ratios also cannot rise or fall indefinitely, so the real GDP growth rate, we argued, is a good proxy for the expected real capital gain of an equity portfolio. Moreover, investors receive dividends and other cash payouts, such as buybacks, and these rewards are in addition to profit growth because they are paid out of profits that are not reinvested in the company. Inflation also must be accounted for. The sum of all of these inputs gives a supply-side estimate of the return available to investors from

---

[1]The historical returns and forecasts were updated on an ongoing basis by Ibbotson Associates, now part of Morningstar.

[2]This necessity is true, at least for equities; for bonds, many of which are issued by governments, the dynamic is different but the money has to be generated by somebody for investors to receive it as a reward for taking risk.

capital markets, which is the aggregation of all the individual security returns addressed by the demand-side approach in the current book.

The authors working with Roger Ibbotson have produced several more articles on the supply model, including a Graham and Dodd Award–winning article by Ibbotson and Chen (2003) and a fine integrative piece by Straehl and Ibbotson (2017).

The Liquidity Factor

With a market price for risk established in *Stocks, Bonds, Bills, and Inflation*, the natural next step was to price the other attributes, such as liquidity (which we called "marketability"), that we identified as affecting asset prices in Ibbotson et al. (1984). In an important precursor to the current book, Ibbotson, Chen, Kim, and Hu (2013) considered one of the factors in isolation: liquidity. Their article asked whether the fact that many investors are averse to illiquidity means that illiquid assets offer superior returns to investors who are not so averse to it. In the abstract of the article, the authors wrote,

> Liquidity should be given equal standing with size, value/growth, and momentum as an investment style . . . [and] is an economically significant indicator of long-run returns. The returns of [the] liquidity [factor] are sufficiently different from those of the other styles that it is not merely a substitute. (p. 30)

The authors back-tested a strategy based on this idea and found large excess returns earned by portfolios of illiquid stocks. By subsuming liquidity into the larger category of popularity—a stock may be popular for many reasons, liquidity being one. In a Graham and Dodd Scroll–winning article, Idzorek, Xiong, and Ibbotson (2012) applied similar concepts to mutual funds. Finally, Ibbotson and Idzorek (2014) and Idzorek and Ibbotson (2017) were the first to specifically name popularity as the embracing concept that includes liquidity and other preference-related factors, arriving at the conceptual framework that is presented in this book.

As IIKX show through empirical tests, popularity is much more than liquidity. It includes such components as brand value, competitive advantage, and reputation as well as more conventional factors, such as high growth rates, profitability, and high beta. All of these attributes, say IIKX, should be avoided by investors seeking above-market returns because assets that have these characteristics are oversubscribed by other investors. By selecting assets with the *opposites* of these characteristics, investors can expect to earn excess returns.

Conclusion: It's Hard but Not Impossible to Beat the Market

Investing in stocks or other assets that most people don't want has a long and rich history, proceeding from Graham and Dodd (1934) through Warren Buffett and many scholars, active managers, hedge fund entrepreneurs, and private equity managers. They all take advantage of some aspect of the popularity hypothesis set forth in this book.

Yet, investing in unpopular assets is hard. First, they are typically unpopular for a reason. Mounting losses instead of bountiful profits, declining market share or a shrinking market for one's product, an unusual loading of debt, and other characteristics that drive investors away are often indicators of continued poor performance rather than of what one value manager optimistically calls "troubles that are temporary." This *value trap* is the pitfall that awaits investors who too blindly follow an unpopularity formula.

Investing in unpopular assets is hard for another reason: Active managers, including those believing themselves to be contrarian, engage in herd behavior. Their quantitative screens all tend to identify the same stocks. If managers focusing on unpopular assets have already formed a cluster of demand for an asset—even if that cluster represents a minority opinion—that asset may no longer be attractively priced.

Following these ideas to their logical conclusion brings the well-known fallacy of aggregation into consideration: Any strategy or factor that is widely enough used will fail. It is easy to imagine so much money flooding into an unpopularity strategy that no unpopular assets exist any longer. If that were to happen, the whole world would become a gigantic closet index fund. We financial economists really do lose sleep over thoughts like that.

Despite these concerns, the market has rewarded value investing and other strategies, such as those advocated in this book, that rely on buying what other investors are avoiding. Value, for example, has won over very long periods of time (back to 1927, according to Eugene Fama and Kenneth French[3]) and by an economically significant margin. But value has not been on top recently; a small number of large and fast-growing companies have increased in relative popularity and beaten almost everything else. Like all other trends in investing, this one will surely turn sooner or later.

Meanwhile, read this book. It returns the CFA Institute Research Foundation, which is proud to present it, to its roots in quantitative financial research while helping to bridge a philosophical divide. And it might contain

---

[3]See French's website: http://mba.tuck.dartmouth.edu/pages/faculty/ken.french/data_library. html.

a key to that most elusive of Greek letters, alpha. Past performance is obviously no guarantee of future results, but it sure is a hint.

Laurence B. Siegel
Gary P. Brinson Director of Research
CFA Institute Research Foundation
July 2018

Preface

The idea that the popularity of an asset affects its pricing, and ultimately its return, is not new but is often overlooked in the mathematics of asset pricing models. Popularity is really just another word for demand, and of course, neo-classical economics—on which standard finance is based—is all about supply and demand. In the short run, the supply of an asset, such as the number of shares of a stock, is relatively fixed. Even when a company is subject to no news, however, the daily price fluctuates. This fluctuation is driven primarily by changes in the demand for the stock.

Popularity can shift daily or even hourly, but it can also be a relatively stable phenomenon. Some companies are inherently attractive or popular, while others remain uninteresting for long periods of time. Some companies have characteristics that investors seem to like, such as a great story behind them with exciting prospects ahead. Other companies plug along with good results but do not inspire the imagination of investors. These boring or even unattractive companies will have lower valuations, and thus higher costs of capital, than the popular companies. We assert it is strategies built on these overlooked stocks, however, even if such strategies appear to underdeliver day to day, that perform the best over the long run.

Recognizing that popularity can affect pricing does not necessarily lead to immediate excess returns. Rather, popularity is usually associated with valuation, an indicator of long-term future performance rather than a predictor of short-term or technical supply/demand imbalances. Benjamin Graham (2006) noted this aspect long ago in his book *The Intelligent Investor*:

> Buying a neglected and therefore undervalued issue for profit generally proves to be a protracted and patience-trying experience. And selling short a too popular and therefore overvalued issue is apt to be a test not only of one's courage and stamina, but also of the depth of one's pocketbook. (pp. 31–32)

This book is based on the insight that Graham and others have always had—namely, that popularity affects security prices and thus expected returns. Whereas Graham focused on mispricing, we focus on long-run premiums. Relative popularity is driven by the collective wisdom—or perhaps not-so-wise collective opinion—of the crowd/investors, so going against the collective wisdom that drives popularity is inherently contrarian. We show that popularity is a broad umbrella under which nearly all market premiums and anomalies, including the classic value and small-cap anomalies, fall. We show this by drawing from both classical and behavioral finance to extend existing asset pricing models to include any security characteristic that investors might care about.

The capital asset pricing model (CAPM), which has dominated finance for the last 50 or more years, is simple and elegant. It is an equilibrium model built on neoclassical economics. From a practitioner perspective, it is extremely simple to apply. The CAPM ignores the insights of behavioral finance, however, and in numerous and systematic ways fails to accurately model asset prices.[4] In this book, we move from an intuitive understanding of popularity to, first, a framework for understanding how popularity predicts the direction of various premiums and anomalies relative to the CAPM and, eventually, to the development of a formal asset pricing model that incorporates the central idea of popularity, which we call the "popularity asset pricing model" (PAPM).

Finally, for the popularity framework to be useful, it should not only be consistent with existing well-known empirical results. It should also predict premiums and anomalies that have not been considered before as priced characteristics. Examples of such characteristics are a company's brand, reputation, and perceived competitive advantage. In this book, we show empirically that these characteristics are priced.

Hence, in both theory and empirical work, this book presents popularity as a bridge between classical and behavioral finance.

---

[4]Although some economists fault the CAPM for its unrealistic assumptions, others—most notably, the late Milton Friedman (1953)—insist that a model should be judged on the power of its predictions, not the realism of its assumptions.

1. Introduction

The existence of various market premiums and anomalies is well established in the finance literature. To date, however, no single agreed-upon explanation for them has emerged. Investment finance is largely divided into two camps, classical and behavioral. Classical finance is based mainly on the idea that investors are risk averse, so market premiums are generally interpreted as risk premiums. In behavioral finance, premiums are considered to be the result of either cognitive errors that investors systematically make or preferences for company or security characteristics that might not be related to risks. We believe that most of the best-known market premiums and anomalies can be explained by an intuitive and naturally occurring (social or behavioral) phenomenon observed in countless settings: popularity.

What Is Popularity?

Popularity is the condition of being admired, sought after, well-known, and/or accepted. A wide range of possible categories—people, food, fashion, music, places to live, types of pet, vacation destinations, television shows, and so on—contain an implicit popularity spectrum or rank. Each of the categories has various criteria for estimating popularity.

For our purposes, the quality of the ranking criteria is not important; what is important is that any given category comprises a natural ordering in which some constituents are more popular than others. Such relative popularity evolves over time. Some aspects of popularity are systematic, or more or less permanent (for example, modern society seems to prefer thin to fat, tall to short). Other aspects of popularity may be transitory or exist only as fads (for example, necktie width, high-waisted jeans, men wearing wigs). Whether the result of systematic trends or idiosyncratic evolution, these rankings are in flux. Some popular items become relatively less popular, and some of the unpopular items become relatively more popular. While unsustainable, some popular items will temporarily become even more popular. For example, liquidity is permanently popular, but on a relative basis during times of market distress, it is especially sought after. Society places a greater relative value (monetary or otherwise) on the more popular items.

In this book, popularity refers to investor preferences—that is, how much an asset is liked or disliked. Of course, the primary preference for investors is to seek returns. Investors do not know what the returns will be, but they can distinguish one asset from another in terms of their observable characteristics, for which they may have clearly defined preferences. Thus, even with the same set of expected cash flows, investors may have more demand for one asset over another, which gives the preferred asset a higher current price and a lower expected return. An asset could be liked (or disliked) for *rational* or *irrational* reasons.[5] In this way, popularity spans ideas from both classical and behavioral finance, thus providing a bridge between the two camps.

In classical finance, the primary preference, beyond maximizing expected return, is to take less risk. This fact has given rise to various models that usually assume no other preferences. In the most well-known model, the capital asset pricing model (CAPM), the only "priced" characteristic is exposure to undiversifiable market risk. We consider a broader set of preferences that lead to other priced characteristics, which might include the rational preferences to reduce catastrophic losses, increase liquidity, be tax efficient, and so on. We also consider preferences that might be more in line with what the literature considers "behavioral," such as desiring to hold companies with strong brands, investments with strong past price increases, or companies that have strong ESG (environmental, social, and governance) characteristics.

The popularity framework presented in this book includes a generalization of a wide range of characteristics in classical finance and behavioral finance that influence how investors value securities. We can classify these characteristics into two broad categories with two subcategories each as follows:

Classical:

1. *Risks.* In classical finance, risk usually refers to fluctuations in asset values, but risk can be interpreted more broadly as any risks to which a rational investor, who assumes away any real-world frictions in the holding and trading of securities, would be averse. Thus, risks may be multidimensional, including various types of stock or bond risks, or may arise from catastrophic events.

2. *Frictional.* These characteristics are often assumed away in classical finance, but a rational investor would consider them. Examples include taxes, trading costs, and asset divisibility.

---

[5]Throughout this book, we describe preferences, or the reasons for preferences, as being either rational or irrational. Rational reasons for preferences are those considered in classical finance, broadly defined. The reasons include expected returns, risk, liquidity, taxes, and trading costs. Generally, rational preferences are pecuniary. Irrational reasons for preferences generally are those identified in behavioral finance and result from the various biases and heuristics identified in that literature. Irrational preferences are generally nonpecuniary. Although Ibbotson, Diermeier, and Siegel (1984) acknowledged the possibility of nonpecuniary security characteristics playing a role in asset pricing (such as in the art market), their focus was on pecuniary characteristics that we consider to be subject to rational preferences. Our popularity framework extends their idea to irrational preferences.

Behavioral:

1. *Psychological.* Investors consider these characteristics because of their psychological impact. For example, buying a company with a small carbon footprint might make an investor feel good.

2. *Cognitive.* Investors consider these factors or fail to accurately interpret such factors because of systematic cognitive errors. For example, investors may overvalue the importance of a company's brand when evaluating its stock because they do not realize that the value of the brand is already embedded in the market price of the stock.

Our fourfold classification of security characteristics partially overlaps with the threefold classification in Statman (2017), in which investors are described as holding securities for utilitarian, expressive, and emotional reasons. Utilitarian reasons correspond to risk and frictional characteristics, and expressive and emotional reasons correspond to psychological characteristics.

In this book, we focus primarily on the stock market, although we believe the concepts can be applied to fixed-income securities, real estate, and numerous other real assets.[6] Periodically, as necessary, we attempt to distinguish between characteristics of a *company* and characteristics of the *security* in question—both of which can have attributes that are more or less popular among investors. Assets are priced not only by their expected cash flows but also by the popularity of the other characteristics associated with the company or security. The less popular stocks have lower prices (relative to the expected discounted value of their cash flows), thus higher expected returns. The more popular stocks have higher prices and, therefore, lower expected returns. Popularity can be related to risk (an unpopular characteristic), and it can also be related to other rational preferences. But popularity can also be related to behavioral concepts. For instance, investors may want to brag about their past winners (or purchase recent winners—for example, in the practice called "window dressing") or hold recognizable securities that are consistent with their social values. Any aspect that can affect the popularity of a stock will affect its demand and thus its price.[7]

Popularity is a bridge between classical finance and behavioral finance because both types of finance rely on preferences. Popularity is an expression of these preferences, whether they are rational, irrational, or somewhere in

---

[6]In Appendix A, we summarize the literature on *psychic return* in art markets, which we interpret to be a *popularity premium.*
[7]By demand, we mean the sum of the demand of all market participants.

between.[8] Popularity does not make a value judgment but, instead, takes preferences as a given and recognizes that preferences can change over time. This book is presented in an equilibrium framework, so asset prices and expected returns reflect the aggregate impact of investor preferences.

Principles and Models of Classical Finance

Classical finance rests on several principles that largely come from economics:

- *Rationality.* This principle states that investors are rational utility maximizers who care about cash flows, expected return, and risk. Although considering liquidity and tax efficiency is also rational, classical finance often assumes away the nonrisk aspects of investments.

- *Risk-free arbitrage.* In economics, this concept is known as "the law of one price."[9] In finance, it specifically means that in the absence of any frictions, such as transaction costs, two securities with the same payouts must have the same price.

- *Equilibrium.* This condition is "supply equals demand." The prices of securities are such that every available share is held by some investor in the quantity that the investor wants to hold at the prevailing prices. A *frictionless* equilibrium has no transaction costs and no risk-free arbitrage opportunities.

- *Efficient markets.* In an efficient market, security prices reflect all relevant information regarding the securities' value. In an efficient market, all prices are "fair"—meaning that they equate to their intrinsic values (which are usually not directly observable) and investors can "beat the market" only through luck or random variation around market benchmarks. As Fama (1970) pointed out, any test of market efficiency must be a test of a joint hypothesis with some other model that explains rational differences in expected returns.

---

[8]The same preference may be rational for one investor and irrational for another investor. For example, it is rational for a taxable investor to consider tax efficiency and irrational for non-taxable investor to seek out tax efficient investments.

[9]In economics, risk-free arbitrage, as defined here, is the only form of true arbitrage. Among investment practitioners, however, the term "arbitrage" is used more broadly to mean going long one security and short another to take advantage of differences in expected returns. An example is going long a value stock and going short a growth stock. As we show in Chapter 5, in equilibrium, an investor may go long an unpopular security and short a popular security, and many practitioners would call this strategy an "arbitrage." However, it is far from risk free. It is sometimes called "speculative arbitrage" (Damodaran).

Models in classical finance generally assume rationality and market efficiency. Where they differ is in whether they assume that risk-free arbitrage eliminates all price discrepancies or whether they make the assumption of equilibrium. The best-known examples of arbitrage models are the arbitrage pricing theory (APT) (Ross 1976) and the Black–Scholes option pricing model (Black and Scholes 1973). Because these models make no direct reference to investors, they make no reference to investor preferences.

The best-known equilibrium model is the CAPM (Sharpe 1964; Lintner 1965; among others). In the CAPM, each investor maximizes a utility function that is higher as expected return increases and lower as variance of return increases. The model takes into account a single preference parameter for risk aversion that identifies how various investors make the trade-off between risk and expected return. In equilibrium, the model assumes a single risk premium, which is a function of the asset-weighted aggregation of the risk aversion parameters.[10]

The practical distinction between arbitrage and equilibrium is in what the two approaches say about prices. Arbitrage models describe the relationships between security prices but do not explain where prices ultimately come from. For example, the Black–Scholes model gives formulas for options on stocks but does not explain how the prices of stocks are determined. The APT, another arbitrage model, says the expected return on a security is a linear function of exposures to a set of factors, with risk premiums on the factors as the coefficients. It does not, however, explain where the risk premiums come from. In contrast, equilibrium models explain security prices in terms of both the characteristics of the securities and the preferences of investors. The CAPM and the popularity asset pricing model (PAPM) that we present in Chapter 5 are equilibrium models.

The New Equilibrium Theory (NET) of Ibbotson, Diermeier, and Siegel (1984; hereafter, IDS) is a precursor to the popularity framework that includes frictional characteristics—such as asset liquidity, taxation, and divisibility—in a general asset pricing framework. These characteristics do not necessarily have to be linear in asset pricing, although for simplicity we specify a model later in this book in which they are. The key is that rational investors have different preferences for these characteristics, making some securities more popular than others. In a rational world, equilibrium prices and expected returns are affected by an asset's frictional characteristics. Although NET was imagined as a potential equilibrium theory, IDS (1984) only outlined what such a

---

[10]We present the formula for the risk premium and other details of the CAPM in Chapter 5 and in detail in Appendix B.

5

theory might look like. In Chapter 5 of this book, we present a fully developed equilibrium asset pricing theory in which investors have preferences for all types of characteristics.

To the extent that an asset's characteristics are permanent and cannot easily be reconstructed or securitized in some form, the disliked characteristics result in expected return premiums that can be predicted over time. An example might be the small-capitalization premium; small-cap stocks are disliked in general because they are riskier and less liquid than large-cap stocks and require more analysis per dollar of investment. If value stocks were permanently unpopular, perhaps because poorly managed or unlucky companies are perceived as poor investments (although we would argue that they can be great investments), they might also receive a long-term premium without being any riskier than growth stocks.

In an equilibrium in which investors have preferences regarding company and security characteristics that are relatively permanent, companies and securities with disliked characteristics will have lower prices and higher expected returns than popular ones, giving rise to what we consider long-term "premiums." In classical finance, the primary disliked characteristic is risk and only the systematic or nondiversifiable part of a security's total risk bears a premium. (Even with rational investors, assets that are difficult to diversify, such as owner-occupied houses or human capital, may have prices that include premiums for idiosyncratic risk.) Furthermore, other characteristics—such as liquidity, taxability, or divisibility—would and should be priced by rational investors.

In this book, we take an equilibrium approach: Investor preferences influence prices and expected returns. In such an equilibrium, natural clienteles may come about in which various investor desires and holdings differ; prices, however, reflect the aggregation of those preferences in the context of the relatively fixed supply of characteristics in the marketplace. The popularity preferences are expressed as demand for those characteristics and an overall demand for expected returns.

Principles of Behavioral Finance

In behavioral finance, individuals suffer from various biases that limit their rationality. Included are many of the biases and heuristics discussed by Tversky and Kahneman (1974), such as the affect heuristic, framing, loss aversion, anchoring, the endowment effect, and overconfidence.

Behavioral economics or behavioral finance is applied in numerous ways. One way is to nudge investors toward better behavior, as suggested by Thaler and Sunstein (2008). Practitioners or academics might develop schemes that help investors save more, plan better for contingencies, and diversify more effectively. In our context, however, we are interested in understanding how investor behavior might affect security prices and returns, not in modifying behavior.

We illustrate in Chapter 5 how, in equilibrium, investor preferences affect security prices and expected returns. In a PAPM illustration, one of the investors is purely rational and cares only about classical characteristics. This investor sees popular securities as being overpriced and takes advantage of this insight by taking levered short positions in those securities and levering up long positions in unpopular securities. The purely rational investor thus influences prices but does not determine them. Therefore, no complete arbitrage takes place in the equilibrium environment because prices reflect the aggregate demand for each security as influenced by all the participants in the market.

We classify the behavior biases or distortions into two distinct types: psychological and cognitive. The psychological biases express desires or needs of the investors; some investors knowingly and willing pay extra to achieve some other good, such as influencing a social goal. The cognitive aspects of behavioral finance usually involve some mistakes investors make, such as overestimating the earnings of a growth company or imagining (against evidence) that momentum will continue.

Demand and Supply

In the primary capital market, companies *demand* capital and, in exchange for the provision of capital, *supply* earnings and, subsequently, cash flows. The cash flows come in the form of dividends, buybacks of shares, cash paid for shares of acquisition targets, and so on. Looking at this process from the other side, investors *supply* capital and *demand* cash flows and returns.

The concept of popularity looks at the market from a *demand* perspective and takes the expected cash flow streams as given. Many investors value a stream by applying a discount rate to it. This discount rate, equivalent to investors' expected return, will be higher or lower depending on the risk, recognizability, liquidity, or general desirability of the stock above and beyond its expected cash flow characteristics. Thus, popularity is a measure of demand: The more demand for a stock, the higher the price and, consequently, the lower the expected return. In the primary capital market, then, capital flows from investors to corporations (through the corporations' costs of capital), which attempt to invest in projects that will generate returns, which enriches corporations and ultimately provides returns back to investors. **Figure 1.1** illustrates these relationships.

In addition to expected returns, investors demand less risk, more liquidity, tax efficiency, dividends, and other desired characteristics. **Figure 1.2** takes these preferences into account.

Figure 1.1. Supply and Demand for Capital and Returns: Flow Chart

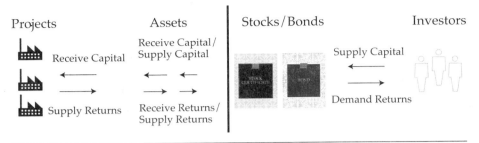

Figure 1.2 depicts the following exchanges between investors and corporations:

- Investors supply capital to the company (the corporate treasury) by purchasing stock and bond issuances (in the primary [direct] capital markets).

- The company (corporate treasury) supplies assets to corporate operations/projects in the form of working capital and assets.

- Corporate operations/projects spend the money in hopes of providing earnings, cash flows, brand power/recognition, and so on, back to the company (corporate treasury).

- The corporate treasury (through its cost of capital) provides returns and cash flow back to stock- and bondholders (which may be the original purchasers from the primary [direct] capital markets or may be acquirers of the securities in the secondary market).

Figure 1.2. Exchanges between Investors and Corporations

	Corporate Operations	Corporate Treasury	Investors

What Is Desired / Demanded?	• From Corporate Treasury
	  • Capital
	  • Assets
		• From Investors
		  • Equity
		  • Debt
		• From Corporate Projects
		  • Earnings
		  • Brand, Reputation, ESG, etc.
			• Expected Returns
			  • Cash Flows/Dividends
			  • Capital Gains
			• Popularity Characteristics
			  • Less Risk
			  • Liquidity
			  • Brand, Reputation, ESG, etc.

What Is Supplied?	• Projects
	  • Earnings
	  • Brand, Reputation, ESG, etc.
		• To Investors
		  • Expected Returns
		  • Popularity Characteristics
		• To Corporate Projects
		  • Capital
		  • Assets
			• Capital
			  • Stocks
			  • Bonds

Although we will focus on the upper right-hand box depicting investor demand for expected returns and security (termed "popularity") characteristics, we recognize that it is corporations that ultimately supply the returns and characteristics through their investments in assets and projects, as expressed through their issuance of debt and equity.

Popularity Premiums

We define a premium as an expected excess return, relative to an appropriate benchmark, that is relatively *permanent* (which we emphasize to distinguish premiums from short-term mispricing). The most clear-cut example is the equity risk premium in which the benchmark is a risk-free asset or a bond index. Stocks are expected to have higher returns than bills and bonds because stocks are riskier. In most cases, risk or uncertainty is undesirable or unpopular. The extra risk or uncertainty in stocks is inherent because, legally, stockholders have a residual claim on a company's cash flows only after all bond interest and principal are paid. Thus, stocks always have positive *expected* excess returns—but not necessarily higher *realized* excess returns, given that uncertain results almost always differ from expectations. The equity risk premium, like any other premium, will be positive in its expectation but, of course, can vary over time as the supply of and demand for capital changes. Over the long run, stocks have indeed had substantially higher returns than bonds or bills.

Risk is only one of many potential reasons that one stock may have a higher expected return than another stock even with similar patterns of expected cash flows. For a return differential to be called a "premium," however, it should not only be permanent and not easily changed, but it should also be relatively consistent over time. For example, some investors will always prefer a liquid investment. Usually, a company cannot easily change the liquidity of its equity. So, the demand for and supply of this liquidity is relatively permanent and will affect a stock's price and expected excess return. The investor willing to invest in the less liquid stock should receive a premium. Arbitrageurs might try to reduce the liquidity premium, perhaps by wrapping illiquid stocks in such a liquid vehicle as an exchange-traded fund, but not all securities can be made uniformly liquid. Thus, like risk, liquidity will be priced in the market.

This book posits a variety of characteristics that might be relatively permanent and are likely to be priced in the stock market. In the CAPM, a security's beta is the only priced characteristic, but in the popularity framework, beta can be either popular or unpopular. The CAPM specifies that the more market or beta risk a security has, the higher its discount rate, the lower its price, and the higher its expected return. Empirical data on individual stocks, however, do not usually support this positive relationship between stock returns and betas. Rather, some analysts have suggested that because the market usually goes up and because investment managers, acting as agents for their investors (customers), want to outperform a majority of the time, these managers may prefer high-beta stocks despite their added extra risk. This phenomenon is a likely explanation of the low-beta anomaly we discuss in Chapter 2.

Other premiums that are generally accepted are size and value. Presumably, all small companies strive to become large companies; however, aspiring and pursuing do not necessarily create reality. Small size is usually a deterrent to institutional investors because it is usually associated with less liquidity, and small-cap stocks generally take more analysis per dollar of investment. Small-cap stocks are also riskier (an unpopular characteristic) than large-cap stocks; thus, the absolute outperformance of small versus large is consistent with the more-risk/more-return CAPM paradigm. Although directionally aligned, the realized premium of small caps has empirically exceeded that which the CAPM would predict.

The value premium is less easily understood, especially from a CAPM perspective, because not much empirical evidence suggests that value stocks are riskier than growth stocks, at least as measured by their standard deviation of returns or CAPM betas. Nevertheless, investors generally think of value stocks as less attractive, perhaps even distressed, companies. Thus, if investors seek growth over value, a value premium will exist in the market. Whether this is a permanent premium is unclear.

Many premiums are not risk based but, rather, are associated with non-risk investor preferences. For example, investors may desire and will pay up for environmentally sensitive companies or those that meet or avoid various social criteria. Companies can, of course, change their ESG policies; in fact, change is what some investors are trying to achieve. But change comes at a cost, and ultimately, investors will have to pay up for these preferences, potentially earning lower returns.

Some preferences are purely behavioral, reflecting preferences that are not risk or return related. For example, investors prefer companies with familiar brands and companies that are successful and have good reputations. All these criteria can make for great companies but not necessarily great investments because the characteristic in question is probably already reflected in the price. Some of these criteria overlap with the criteria by which value companies are judged (e.g., value companies may have weak brands or produce items the general public does not appreciate), which may partially explain why value stocks earn a premium. Of course, even though companies usually want to improve their situations, brands and reputations and core product offerings are not easily changed. Value companies might wish to become growth companies to become more desirable to investors, but here again, a stock's classification is not easily changed on the supply side, nor is investor excess demand for growth likely to disappear.

In some time periods, popular stocks become even more popular and temporarily outperform less popular stocks, such as the five-year period preceding the dot-com crash. In all the cases that we discuss, however, over reasonably long periods of time, the less popular stocks have earned premiums. This result may be counterintuitive, but we demonstrate it empirically in Chapters 6 and 7.

Premiums vs. Mispricing

The notion of mispricing requires the existence of a "true price" from which the price has diverged. Such a true price can never be known, so to declare any particular security to be "mispriced" is daring. If a true price were known and the price had, in fact, diverged from this price, the market would be in a state of disequilibrium with numerous investors trying to either buy or short the mispriced security (i.e., not every market participant would be able to hold the desired shares).

Practitioners frequently use the term "mispriced" to describe a security that they believe (but do not know with certainty) has diverged from what they believe to be something akin to the true price. This usage simply reflects different opinions about expected returns and other preferences; it does not represent true mispricing and is consistent with market equilibrium (i.e., every market participant is able to hold the desired shares). For example, like all models, the CAPM is a crude model of reality. It produces an expected return, and hence an estimate of price, that in most cases is wrong. So, one might say a security is mispriced *relative to* the price given by the CAPM. To repeat, the CAPM may be wrong and the market may be in equilibrium.

Because most of the premiums we discuss are relatively permanent, we do not consider that the differential returns various clienteles can expect to earn are market inefficiencies. Rather, they are the premium payoffs for the willingness to invest in stocks that other investors want to avoid or underweight in an equilibrium setting. The investors with strong preferences might be called "the willing losers" or, in some cases, "unknowing losers."[11] They allow other investors to earn excess returns by taking on more risk, tolerating less liquidity, having longer time horizons, or investing in companies that are shunned by others. The investors with weaker preferences (even if the preferences are in the same direction) should expect to earn higher returns, even in equilibrium.

Various investor portfolios will have different returns from one another, even over the long run. There are three possible explanations:

1. Long-term premiums—portfolios have risk premiums and other types of premiums.

2. Luck—investors were lucky or unlucky.

3. Skill—investors skillfully bought and sold the mispriced securities at the appropriate times (or had perverse skill and did the opposite).

The first and second explanations are consistent with efficient markets. The third explanation involves mispricing and inefficient markets. Mispricing, by its very nature, must be relatively short term because the skilled investor can benefit from the distortions only if prices tend to correct themselves.

To sum up, popularity can be viewed from both a classical and a behavioral perspective and can include both long-term premiums and mispricing.

Popularity and Adaptive Markets

Andrew Lo (2017) has written a book about how ideas and markets evolve under changing economic, behavioral, and technological circumstances. Although Lo does not use the term "popularity," his approach is consistent with ours. His focus is on the dynamics of financial thought over time.

Investors, markets, and products adapt, but the economic environment is also continually changing. As imperfect beings, we never fully reach the classical ideal, and although we learn, we cannot fully dissociate ourselves from our evolutionary selves in purely rational ways. Some assets will always be more popular than others, for both rational and irrational reasons. In adaptive markets, premiums may shift over time, prices may be corrected, but new pricing discrepancies may be introduced.

Although our book is broad, it is more limited in scope than Lo's (2017) *Adaptive Markets*. We focus on investor demand to show how investor preferences can be characterized by the popularity of various assets and

---

[11]The phrase "willing loser" comes from a quote of Robert Arnott in Rostad (2013). Here we are coining the phrase "unknowing loser."

premiums. The returns we measure are long term and span decades, but they do not span the centuries and millennia that Lo addresses. Our premiums adapt over time, but that change is not our main emphasis. Rather, we are trying to characterize why the premiums exist. We set out to understand how prices are formed in a market environment made up of investors with both rational and irrational preferences. Both Lo's and our approaches help bridge the gap between classical and behavioral finance.

2. Premiums, Anomalies, and Popularity

Popularity provides an explanation for the relative performance of different asset classes and different securities.[12] Asset pricing theories have long recognized that expected returns should not be the same for instruments in the marketplace that have different characteristics. The primary explanation for these differences has been differences in risk. Of course, risk is unpopular: Investors do not like risk and want to be compensated for it. But other characteristics matter too.

For a given security or asset class, the capital asset pricing model (CAPM), which is an equilibrium model, splits risk into two parts: the beta (or systematic or market risk) and the residual (or diversifiable risk). According to the CAPM, only the beta part of the risk should be compensated with higher expected returns because the residual risk can easily be eliminated by diversification but systematic risk cannot be diversified away. Other theories, such as the arbitrage pricing theory (an arbitrage model) developed by Ross (1976), posit multiple risk factors that bear premiums.

Following the publication of Fama and French (1992), although even before that time, size and value became generally accepted as additional risk factors for the stock.[13] Fama and French originally characterized size and value as "risk" premiums, even though little evidence exists that value is associated with risk, as measured by volatility. If one were forced to attempt to explain the value premium as a risk premium, one might focus on the expectation of an increased risk of bankruptcy or having financial distress that manifests itself when investors are most vulnerable, in which the higher risk of bankruptcy at the macro level has yet to be realized in the data series most often studied.

Other characteristics were also recognized as affecting returns. For some time, we have known that liquidity affects bond yields and that investors demand the expectation of a premium to lock up their capital in real estate or private equity, which are illiquid. Amihud and Mendelson (1986), among others, showed that liquidity also affects stocks. Ibbotson, Chen, Kim, and Hu (2013) demonstrated that liquidity could be considered a style factor

---

[12]This chapter is partially based on Ibbotson and Idzorek (2014) and Idzorek and Ibbotson (2017).

[13]Fama and French (1992) was integrative rather than original. The size effect was discovered by Banz (1981) and Reinganum (1981), and the value effect was discovered by Basu (1977). Sharpe (1988, 1992) developed returns-based style analysis as a factor model that included size and value factors before Fama and French (1992) developed their factor model of size and value.

because liquidity premiums appear to be at least comparable to size or value premiums. Building on stock-level liquidity premiums, Idzorek, Xiong, and Ibbotson (2012) found that after controlling for other characteristics, mutual funds that, on average, held the less liquid stocks outperformed—even net of fees. Liquidity can be cast as the risk of not being able to turn your investment into cash extremely quickly without a price concession.

Another factor that might affect stock returns is momentum. Jegadeesh and Titman (1993) suggested that momentum affects stocks because they found that stocks that have performed well in the previous 12 months appear to do better than those that performed relatively poorly. The momentum anomaly has been more erratic over more recent periods; much of the research since 1993 has attempted to understand how and why momentum seems to have worked. Xiong and Ibbotson (2015) showed that stocks that have accelerating prices are more likely to have poor returns and crash.

Asset Class Risks

Across the asset classes, Ibbotson and Sinquefield (1976a) measured various types of risk premiums, including the equity risk premium and small-cap premium for stocks and the horizon risk (maturity) premium and default premium for bonds. When added to the base of expected inflation and real (inflation-adjusted) interest rates, Ibbotson and Sinquefield (1976b) formed forecasts of returns for the stock and bond asset classes. The expectation of higher returns for stocks than bonds was explained by the fact that stocks are much riskier than bonds. Furthermore, small-cap stocks are riskier than large-cap stocks and longer-term bonds. Those with default risk are riskier than shorter-term bonds and those with less default risk. **Table 2.1** shows

Table 2.1.   Stocks, Bonds, Bills, and Inflation: Summary Statistics of Annual Total Returns, 1926–2017

Asset Class	Geometric Mean (%)	Arithmetic Mean (%)	Standard Deviation (%)
Large-cap stocks	10.2	12.1	19.8
Small-cap stocks	12.1	16.5	31.7
Long-term US government bonds	5.5	6.0	9.9
Intermediate US government bonds	5.1	5.2	5.6
US Treasury bills	3.4	3.4	3.1
Inflation	2.9	3.0	4.0

Source: Ibbotson (2018).

the results of the Ibbotson and Sinquefield approach updated for the period 1926–2017.

Figure 2.1 provides a plot of the annual geometric local currency real returns and standard deviations associated with stocks, bonds, and Treasury bills for 19 countries from 1901 through 2017 based on data from Dimson, Marsh, and Staunton (2002) and updated through 2017. The Dimson et al. data set includes 21 countries, but we omitted Germany and Austria because of their incomplete or extreme returns associated with World Wars I and II.

For the three asset classes (stocks, bonds, and bills), the risk–return paradigm appears to work reasonably well—that is, a regression line passed through *all* of the data points results in the expected positive slope.

Figure 2.1. Risk and Return of Stocks, Bonds, and Government Bills of 19 Countries: 1901–2017

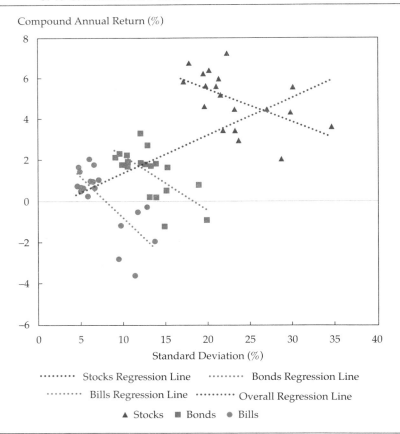

Source: Dimson et al. (2002) updated through 2017 with data from Morningstar Direct.

In contrast, if one passes a regression line separately through each of the asset classes, for all the countries, the relationship within all three asset classes is somewhat negative, suggesting that risk is the dominant factor *among* different asset classes but not *within* an asset class.

The Equity Premium

First and foremost of the risk premiums is the equity risk premium. The additional risk of equities relative to safer investments represents an unpopular characteristic, so the positive equity premium is consistent with the idea of popularity. The notion of an equity or market risk premium was explicitly defined and modeled by Williams (1938) and robustly measured on an ongoing basis starting with Ibbotson and Sinquefield (1976a). That equities are riskier than bonds makes intuitive sense; therefore, equities should carry the expectation of a return premium that compensates the investor for the increased risk.[14] The market (equity risk) premium is the key input in the CAPM. Under the CAPM, as long as the market risk premium is expected to be positive, more risk (market beta) results in greater expected return.

Popularity and the Equity Premium Puzzle. Mehra and Prescott (1985) coined the expression "equity premium puzzle" and argued that the equity premium has been too large relative to academic models of investor behavior, including the CAPM. They maintained that the observed historical equity premium is consistent with relative risk aversion that is approximately 30 times greater than theoretical estimates. Working with a version of Kahneman and Tversky's (1979) *prospect theory* (in which losses hurt far more than equivalent gains help), Benartzi and Thaler (1995) claimed to have solved the equity premium puzzle. Mehra and Prescott (2003) reviewed the various explanations for why the equity premium has been so large, including Benartzi and Thaler's, and concluded that the equity premium remains a puzzle.

Ang (2014, pp. 242–52) provided an overview of the four primary explanations for the equity premium puzzle: Aversion to market risk is sometimes very high (Campbell and Cochrane 1999), disaster risk is feared (Rietz 1988; Jorion and Goetzmann 1999), long-run risk is undesirable (Bansal and Yaron 2004), and investors are heterogeneous (Jerison 1984; Kirman 2006).[15]

---

[14]Goetzmann and Ibbotson (2008) chronicled the history of the concept of an equity premium, documenting that it was not until the 1930s that economists developed a clear conception of the equity risk premium. In a literature review, Siegel (2017) further explored the history and current status of this concept.

[15]Heterogeneous investors play an important role in the popularity asset pricing model we present in Chapter 5.

Interestingly, while discussing the risk-free-rate puzzle of Weil (1989), Ang stated, "It turns out that the question, 'why are equity returns so high?' is the flip side of the question, 'why are risk-free rates so low?'" (p. 245).

Idzorek (2015) offered a popularity-based explanation for the yin and yang of the risk-free and equity premium puzzles:

> [E]quity investing has been substantially democratized—with the creation of the first modern mutual fund in the 1920s, steady decreases in trading costs, the first index funds in the 1970s, and more recently the advent of exchange-traded funds. This democratization has increased equity investing's relative popularity. An increase in its popularity seems to have corresponded with a substantial return premium over bonds. (p. 48)

That is, a long, steady increase in the relative popularity of equity investing may have contributed to the high *realized*, historical equity premium (demand increasing faster than supply). In the future, unless further gains in the popularity of equity investing occur, the expected equity premium is likely to be lower than it has been. This explanation would also imply that the equity premium is not the result of a stationary process.

Goetzmann and Ibbotson (2008) documented the historical equity premium in the United States between 1792 and 1925 and between 1926 and 2004. They found a significantly higher realized premium between 1926 and 2004. Proving that the democratization of equity investing contributed to the increased realized historical equity premium would be difficult, but the relationship seems plausible. Consistent with the shifting relative popularity of stocks versus bonds, nearly 90 years ago Fisher (1930) wrote,

> . . . investment trusts and investment council tend to diminish the risk to the common stock investor. This new movement has created a new demand for such stocks and raised their prices, at the same time it has tended to decrease the demand for, and to lower the price of, bonds. (p. 221)

Fisher (1930) made this observation during a time of euphoric stock market popularity. Almost three-quarters of a century later, Duca (2001) chronicled the further democratization of the US capital markets, including an increase in the number of households owning stock, which went from 25% in the 1960s to 50% in the 1990s.

Premiums and Anomalies within Equity Markets

Although risk may be the main driver of return differences *among* asset classes (bills vs. bonds, bonds vs. stocks, and so on, as illustrated in Figure 2.1), increasing evidence indicates that risk is not the primary driver *within* asset classes. Frazzini and Pedersen (2014) and others demonstrated that in the

Figure 2.2.   Risk and Return for Factor-Based Equity Portfolios, 1972–2016

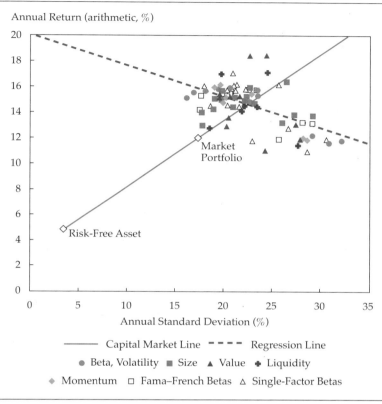

Sources: Ibbotson and Kim (2017); Ibbotson (2018).

equity asset class, low-beta and low-volatility portfolios have done better than high-beta or high-volatility portfolios, which Asness, Frazzini, and Pedersen (2012) attributed to leverage aversion. Ibbotson and Kim (2017) showed that the risk and return dimensions are surprisingly reversed for most of the factors that affect stock returns. We show this result in **Figure 2.2.**[16]

To some degree, Figure 2.2 focuses on a single plot point from Figure 2.1: US equities. In the US equity asset class, sorts based on beta, volatility; size of companies measured by accounting data; value measures; momentum; various factor loadings; and so on show the seemingly perverse result that

---

[16]Figure 2.2 is Figure 9 in Ibbotson and Kim (2017). It is a plot of the results for all the equity portfolios that are based on such factors as size, value, and liquidity. We present these results for many of these portfolios in Chapter 7.

within the US stock market, the lower risk characteristics are associated with higher returns. The regression line in Figure 2.2 depicts this result. This line is in contrast to the capital market line, which is positively sloped and runs through the points representing the market portfolio and the risk-free asset.[17]

If risk is not the single driver of returns, what is? Investors do not like risk. Therefore, they need to be compensated for taking on risk, especially for the betas or systematic risks that they cannot collectively avoid. Unfortunately, the term "risk" has become a catch-all for any attribute that investors do not like even though the attribute may not be directly linked to risk.

The compensation for risk makes sense, but compensation should also apply to other characteristics that investors do not like. Asset prices should also reflect the characteristics that investors like "too much." Stated simply and broadly, if an asset has characteristics that investors really like, its price will be high. If the asset has characteristics that investors do not like, its price will be low, all other things being equal. Thus, the asset with the more desirable characteristics should have lower expected relative returns, whereas the asset with less desirable characteristics should have higher expected relative returns.

Risk is only one dimension of popularity. Popularity can include all sorts of other characteristics that do not fit well into the risk–return paradigm. Following the preference for less risk, the next most obvious characteristic that investors nearly uniformly desire is liquidity. For a given level of expected return and risk, investors prefer high liquidity.

Just as avoiding risk is not free, however, neither is avoiding illiquidity. Both often come at the expense of lower expected returns. Assets with high liquidity are coveted and thus more expensive than assets with low liquidity, even though the differences in liquidity or transaction costs might appear minor. Liquidity cannot easily be squeezed into a risk–return paradigm because the less liquid assets are not necessarily more volatile, nor do they necessarily have higher betas.

Less liquid assets are not usually more volatile, so they are not riskier by that measure.[18] Less liquid investments may involve the risk, however, that one cannot sell (before the investment matures, if it ever does) without suffering delays or being forced to make substantial price concessions. Thus,

---

[17]The market portfolio is the cap-weighted benchmark in Ibbotson and Kim (2017), which consists of all stocks in their universe. The risk-free asset is the 30-day US T-bill from Ibbotson (2018), with the monthly returns linked to form annual returns.

[18]A liquidity factor is sometimes constructed, as in Pástor and Stambaugh (2003). Even though the factor itself is volatile and different stocks have different covariances with it, this aspect does not imply that the less liquid components of the factor are more volatile than the more liquid components.

liquidity is very popular and likely to remain so. All else being equal, high liquidity is more expensive than low liquidity. Low liquidity lowers valuations but raises expected returns.

Strategies that involve buying stocks that are too popular should have lower returns than strategies that buy less popular stocks. By its nature, a strategy that focuses on buying the less popular stocks will be contrarian. Investors will have to go against the crowd.

The liquidity effect illustrates that once we go beyond the risk–return paradigm, we can better understand the various anomalies and premiums found in the marketplace. Investors can have reasons to dislike an asset other than it being too risky. They can also have reasons to like an asset other than it having low risk. We associate *liking* with popularity and *disliking* with unpopularity.

Now consider the generally accepted premiums in asset prices.[19] These premiums are considered systematic; that is, they are more or less permanent in nature. Each of the premiums is associated with something that investors do not like. Once they are discovered, many anomalies are no longer priced. Premiums remain priced, however, because investors might not like characteristics even if they understand that they are paying for them. In such a case, these premiums continue to exist in equilibrium.

Size Premium. Banz (1981) identified the *size* or *small-cap premium*. Like the equity premium, the size premium may be directly related to risk because, on average, small-cap companies are less stable and have more volatile stock prices than large-cap companies. In addition to having higher risk, small-cap stocks are usually less liquid, are less well covered by analysts (have higher research costs), and have lower investment capacity than large-cap stocks. If one thinks of the amount invested as a relative popularity vote, then by definition, small-cap stocks are unpopular relative to large-cap stocks.

Following this logic, mega-cap companies are more popular than large-cap companies and so on until small-cap companies are more popular than microcap companies. In **Figure 2.3**, we reproduce an exhibit from Ibbotson (2018) that shows a monotonic relationship between size decile and realized return: The decile of largest companies (#1) has the lowest arithmetic average annual realized return and systematic risk (beta), and as we move along the size decile spectrum from #1 to #10, we see average return and systematic risk steadily increase.

---

[19]We limited ourselves to equity-oriented premiums and anomalies, but both the horizon (duration or maturity) premium and the credit (default) premium are consistent with the popularity framework.

Figure 2.3. Security Market Line and Scatterplot of Arithmetic Average Total Return of the CRSP/NYSE/NASDAQ Size Deciles, 1926–2017

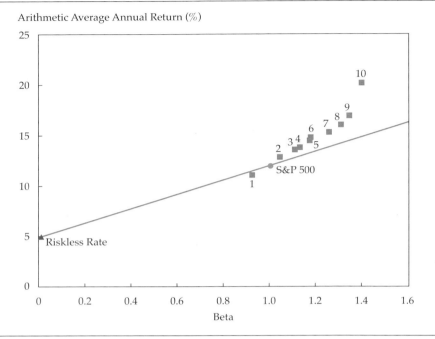

Note: CRSP is the Center for Research in Security Prices.
Source: Ibbotson (2018).

Value Premium. One of the original and most significant cracks in the CAPM and risk–return paradigm came with the publication of work by Basu (1977) that documented the "value effect." Basu found that portfolios of value stocks (stocks with low price–earnings ratios) dramatically outperform portfolios of growth stocks (stocks with high price–earnings ratios), with less risk.[20] Thus, calling a return premium a *risk premium* is not necessarily correct. Subsequent authors have documented the value premium in various time periods and markets and by using various measures of value.

Academicians continue to debate potential explanations for the value premium. Lakonishok, Shleifer, and Vishny (1994) argued that the value

---

[20]In early studies of the value effect, such as Basu (1977), researchers used a single metric, such as price-to-earnings and price-to-book, as the sorting variable. Since then, index providers have developed multifactor models to classify stocks along the value/growth spectrum. These factors include both price ratios and growth measures such as analysts' expected earnings growth rates.

premium (or "glam[orous] stock discount") is the result of systematic suboptimal behavior by typical investors springing from their consistent overconfidence about, and overestimation of, the future growth of earnings and cash flows. Anginer and Statman (2010) offered evidence that the names of some companies elicit a positive reaction, leading investors to wrongly associate them with higher expected future returns.

Most of these explanations are consistent with the popularity perspective: If growth companies are popular and value companies are unpopular, for whatever reason, then growth stocks will be relatively higher priced relative to value stocks. If this popularity is somewhat permanent, we can think of these as premiums rather than as mispricing.

Liquidity Premium. Liquidity does not require a behavioral explanation, but as noted previously, it is consistent with popularity. Rational investors want more liquidity, so investors with longer horizons who do not seek liquidity in the short run earn a liquidity premium. Liquidity has a number of potential measures that are likely to capture somewhat different characteristics. Using bid–ask spreads to proxy liquidity, Amihud and Mendelson (1986) documented that less liquid stocks outperform more liquid stocks. Haugen and Baker (1996) and Datar, Naik, and Radcliffe (1998) showed that low-turnover stocks earn higher future returns than high-turnover stocks.

Ibbotson et al. (2013) demonstrated that investing in the less liquid securities could result in a premium that is at least comparable to the size and value premiums. Building on stock-level liquidity premiums, Idzorek et al. (2012), as noted earlier, found that after they controlled for other characteristics, mutual funds that held the less liquid stocks outperformed, net of fees. From a popularity perspective, all else being equal, investors clearly prefer greater liquidity. However, there is a tight relationship between liquidity and size. Again, securities with the unpopular characteristic have outperformed those with the popular characteristic.

Severe Downside-Risk Premium. The severe downside-risk premium is consistent with the idea of popularity. Kraus and Litzenberger (1976) demonstrated that because investors do not like stocks with severe downside risk (negative coskewness), these stocks have higher returns. This phenomenon is directly related to prospect theory posited by Kahneman and Tversky (1979). In this application of the theory, losses hurt far more than equivalent gains help, particularly when assessed relative to an investor's starting position. Harvey and Siddique (2000) showed that coskewness (one measure of severe downside risk) has earned a significant premium, averaging approximately 3.6% per year for US stocks.

Low-Volatility and Low-Beta Anomalies. Clarke, de Silva, and Thorley (2011), Baker and Haugen (2012), Ang (2014), Blitz and van Vliet (2007), Frazzini and Pedersen (2014), and others have contributed to the growing empirical documentation of the low-volatility and low-beta anomalies. Haugen and Heins (1975) first documented that high risk (volatility and systematic risk) does not necessarily lead to high returns within the universe of equities.

Possibly, restrictions on leverage or a general aversion to leverage, as put forth initially by Black (1972) and more recently by Asness et al. (2012), reverse the expected relationship between risk and return.[21] Also, Baker, Bradley, and Wurgler (2011) suggested that institutional active equity fund managers intentionally seek a beta greater than 1.0 in hopes of frequently outperforming their benchmarks/peer groups, even if this strategy ends up hurting their long-term beta-adjusted performance (alpha). Similarly, we argue that active equity managers, in their quest for outperformance (primarily in absolute terms—that is, not risk adjusted), purposely seek out holdings with high volatility. Hence, both high-beta stocks and high-volatility stocks are the most popular stocks; thus, both low-beta stocks and low-volatility stocks are the least popular stocks, leading to their higher relative returns.

In most cases in which an investor has decided to invest with a particular equity investment manager (mutual fund), the investor has knowingly signed up for a risky investment—presumably, in hopes of realizing an expected return premium. And if the investors are paying for active management, they are also hoping for better-than-market performance. For reasons that are beyond the scope of this book, in this context, investors seem to care more about absolute return and return relative to peer groups than they care about risk-adjusted return.

The typical active investment manager knows that the way to gather more assets is to outperform, in absolute terms, similar competing investment managers. In a quest to outperform on an absolute basis in a world in which leverage is typically off the table, this quest creates a supersized demand for high-beta stocks. In an odd equilibrium sense, this reduces the

---

[21]Black (1972) showed that if we drop the assumption that all investors can borrow and lend at the same riskless rate without limit, the expected return on a portfolio of risky assets that has a beta of zero replaces the risk-free rate in the CAPM equation for expected return. Consequently, if the expected return of the zero-beta portfolio is greater than the risk-free rate (that is, if the CAPM line is flatter than the original CAPM predicts), low-beta stocks will have positive alphas and high-beta stocks will have negative alphas in the standard CAPM. Hence, Black's version of the CAPM provides an explanation for the low-beta anomaly that is not based on behavioral finance.

realized returns of high-beta stocks to a level lower than that which would be predicted by the CAPM so that the equities in question will unequivocally underperform on a risk-adjusted basis but may be able to slightly outperform on an absolute basis; hence, the higher demand.

The Momentum Anomaly. Consistent with the idea of mispricing, past winners seem to continue to win for a period of time. Such *momentum* should not be thought of as a premium but, rather, as characterizing a transition period during which a change in valuation is slowly (and somewhat predictably) taking place. The change can be caused by either changing popularity or a delayed reaction to changing fundamentals, but in either case, a behavioral model is needed to account for the momentum anomaly.

For example, momentum may be the result of an attention-causing event that creates more interest in a stock and/or an increase in trading activity. An increase in trading activity, and thus liquidity, coincides with a price increase, an increase in market capitalization, and probably more attention to the stock, increased liquidity, and further price increases—all part of a temporary, but unsustainable, virtuous circle. Should the price exceed that which is justified by the company's fundamentals, the stock in question peaks in popularity. The degree to which the security is mispriced is noticed by more and more market participants, including short sellers. Then, the momentum ends. The price stagnates and eventually begins to fall. A vicious circle starts that eventually, although it may temporarily overshoot, returns the price to a more "reasonable" level.

ESG Premiums and Discounts. We use the term "environmental, social, and governance" (ESG) as an overall bucket that includes the stocks of companies that score well on ESG criteria, includes the stocks of companies that pass socially responsible investing (SRI) screens, and excludes so-called sin stocks. This bucketing limits the scope of our analysis, because clearly ESG is a multifaceted area worthy of further analysis elsewhere. Sin stocks are offered by companies/industries that people tend to dislike—for example, companies associated with tobacco, alcohol, firearms, and weapons. SRI seeks to explicitly avoid such sin stocks, and ESG-oriented investing usually strikes a balance by rating investments on the basis of various SRI attributes and showing preference for the higher rated stocks. In contrast with SRI, ESG investing does not avoid entire industries but tilts toward companies rated high on the ESG scales.

Relating specifically to sin stocks, Hong and Kacperczyk (2009) studied returns from 1965 to 2006 and found that sin stocks produced a substantial annual alpha slightly greater than 300 basis points. They argued that sin stocks attract fewer institutional investors and less analyst coverage. Return patterns among ESG investing is mixed (see Statman and Glushkov 2011). As with our explanation based on popularity, behavioral economists attribute the sin stock premium to affect, or judgments about good or bad feelings, experienced in relation to the investment in question.

Competitive Advantage, Brand, and Company Reputation. Given popularity's ability to explain most of the well-known premiums and anomalies, we have been searching for characteristics that align with an intuitive definition of popularity to see if we can find further evidence to support or contradict the popularity framework. In Chapter 6, we present our findings for three dimensions of popularity: sustainable competitive advantage, brand, and reputation. (Of these, company reputation is arguably closely linked to ESG.) Overall, we found that quartiles containing the least popular stocks—as represented by low/no sustainable competitive advantage, relatively low brand power, and relatively low company reputation—nearly monotonically produced returns superior to ensuing quartiles of more popular stocks.

Lack of attention is a behavior that probably contributes to the popularity premiums associated with competitive advantage, brand, and company reputation. Barber and Odean (2008) found that investors often limit their opportunity set to stocks that have caught their attention. They concluded that the "utility of an alternative is affected by how many agents choose that alternative. Thus, the attention attracting qualities of an alternative may indirectly detract from its utility" (pp. 812–813). Growth stocks appear to generate more attention than value stocks.

Exhibit 2.1 summarizes the various premiums/anomalies and the respective summary popularity-based explanations that we discussed in this chapter.

Other Premiums and Anomalies. Many more premiums exist than just the few we listed in this chapter. In fact, so many have been identified that Cochrane (2011) refers to a "zoo of new factors" (p. 1047). Green, Hand, and Zhang (2017) listed almost 100 potential factors, and Harvey, Liu, and Zhu (2016) listed more than 300 factors identified in the financial literature as providing high returns. Of course, the authors point out that the factors are cross-correlated and can be categorized into subgroups. Also, many appear to arise from after-the-fact data mining, so the hurdle rate for accepting them as premiums should be high.

In this chapter, we focused on the premiums that are generally recognized by the academic community. One could reasonably question our selected set, because they are primarily the premiums that were discovered the earliest rather than the set of premiums that have the most statistical significance. Our most important criterion for inclusion, however, was that each

Exhibit 2.1. Popularity-Based Explanations of Premiums and Anomalies

Premium/Anomaly Characteristic or Dimension of Popularity	Popularity-Based Explanation
Equity premium	Stocks are riskier than safe assets. Risk is unpopular.
Size	Small-cap stocks are riskier than large-cap stocks. They are also less liquid, less well covered, and have lower investment capacity.
Value	Value stocks are often out of favor (unpopular), are less well-known, and/or operate in the less glamorous industries.
Liquidity	Investors prefer more liquidity to less.
Severe downside risk	Investors dislike large losses.
Low volatility/beta	Active managers prefer high-beta stocks in hopes of outperforming benchmarks.
Momentum	Attention-causing events create interest, which increases trading activity and liquidity and results in an unsustainable virtuous mispricing circle.
ESG	Investors tend to avoid sin stocks and seek out responsible investments.
Competitive advantage, brand, and reputation	Stocks of companies with desirable attributes—competitive advantage, brand power, or company reputation—are sought out beyond their economic benefits.

Source: Based on Exhibit 1 in Idzorek and Ibbotson (2017).

premium have some economic explanation. For us, this explanation is related to popularity.

Conclusion

In this chapter, we examined some of the well-known premiums and anomalies and found that all are consistent with the direction predicted by popularity: Those that embody a more-or-less permanent unpopular characteristic have been rewarded with a popularity premium. Characteristics that rapidly change in popularity can result in mispricing, especially to the extent that the popularity changes are predictable.

Except for the momentum and low-beta/low-volatility anomalies, most of the premiums we examined are thought by some researchers to be consistent with efficient markets, probably because they have been considered risk premiums. What is becoming increasingly clear from empirical results, however, is that many of the premiums are not associated with extra risk and, in some cases, are associated with a risk reduction. Thus, we need popularity to explain not only the premiums but also many of the anomalies that we observe in capital markets. In the following chapters, we show how popularity does so.

Appendix A. Psychic Returns in Art Markets

Popularity is a social phenomenon associated with being admired, sought after, well-known, and so forth. Art collecting and investing can shed some light on the popularity hypothesis. What drives passionate collectors or art investors is the individual interpretation of artwork. Unlike stocks, art has no balance sheet, cash flow, or earnings to help determine its value. The valuation of art is almost entirely subjective.

Baumol (1986) calculated the returns in the art market over three centuries (1650–1960) and found that the average annual real (inflation-adjusted) return was about 0.55%. Thus, he called investing in art a "floating crap game" (p. 10). He reported that the real return on bonds over the study period was about 2.5%. Given that art as an investment provides much lower returns than stocks and bonds, in line with the equilibrium approach and the no arbitrage conditions in financial economics, Baumol's findings suggest that the difference (1.95 percentage points) must be attributed to nonpecuniary returns or the utility derived from the aesthetic pleasure in art investments. In other words, art owners are willing losers from a financial return perspective because they derive utility from art. From this perspective, even though the investors own the art, it is almost as if they are paying a rental fee.

Spaenjers, Goetzmann, and Mamonova (2015) argued that to understand the economics of the market for art, one needs to examine the formation of art prices on a disaggregated level. Each individual piece of artwork gives rise to a market for trading in its private-value benefits (or nonfinancial utility). Within this framework, they discussed recent theoretical and empirical studies of the various forces driving the willingness to pay of bidders at art auctions. Emerging conclusions of this body of work are that the enjoyment associated with art ownership is multifaceted and that preferences interact with wealth in determining the magnitude of private values.

Therefore, the total returns of art investments can be decomposed into two components: psychic (or nonfinancial) returns and financial returns. The psychic returns include, but are not limited to, aesthetic returns and any other prestige and complementarity effects. To some extent, psychic returns are popularity premiums—that is, the premiums paid for pleasure and enlightenment, being admired or sought after. Financial returns relate to the change in the price of the art objects. The price changes can be actual market prices or changes in expert opinions. Financial returns are easier to quantify, of course, than psychic returns.

The key question is *how* to quantify the psychic returns. Much debate is going on in cultural economics about how to measure the psychic returns of art investments. The literature provides three ways to estimate the psychic returns in the art market: Jensen's alpha, rental charge, and opportunity cost.

Jensen's Alpha. Stein (1977) proposed that Jensen's alpha should be taken as a measure of the returns from the viewing of an artwork. Chanel, Gérard-Varet, and Ginsburgh (1994) and Hodgson and Vorkink (2004) also associated the alpha estimate in the single-factor market model with a measure of psychic returns in art market investments.

This framework is based on the market model. In the market model, the returns on all securities are from two sources—a single market factor and idiosyncratic return. The result is the following regression equation:

$$R_a - R_f = \alpha + \beta(R_m - R_f) + \varepsilon,$$

where

R_a = return series on art investments
R_f = return series on a risk-free asset
R_m = return series on the market portfolio
β = sensitivity of the excess returns on art investment to the excess returns on the market portfolio
α = the part of the excess returns on an art investment that cannot be explained by its risk–return relationship with the market portfolio
ε = residual unsystematic and diversifiable risk

The psychic return is defined as the negative of Jensen's alpha (i.e., $-\alpha$). The logic is that if the investor had chosen to invest in securities with no psychic return instead of art, he or she would have earned a financial return higher by the amount of the alpha.

Empirical analyses typically estimate α to be negative, so psychic returns are positive. For example, Stein's (1977) point estimate of α is −1.6%. Pesando (1993) studied the returns in the market for prints for the period 1972–1992 and separately examined returns on Picasso prints. Pesando's estimation results for the market model yielded an α of −1.5% for the overall market for prints and an α of −1.2% for Picasso prints. Chanel et al. (1994) estimated the values of α to be close to −1.0%. Hodgson and Vorkink (2004) reported an estimate for α of −0.8%. In summary, when the market model framework is used, the estimated psychic return is in the range of 1%–2%.

Rental Charge. Renting or leasing a piece of art provides possession of the object without having ownership. Thus, the renter is not concerned with any changes in its market price. The renter is solely paying for viewing the object and enjoying any other intangible returns it yields.

Atukeren and Seçkin (2007) argued that the psychic returns from investing in artwork are the changes in their rental prices. The authors made use of the prices charged by a Canadian fine art company for its art rental services and calculated the implied psychic returns to be about 28% of the sale price (hammer price) in international auctions. In an alternative way, they followed Hodgson and Vorkink's (2004) suggestion that the Jensen's alpha captures the extent of net psychic returns. The evidence for alpha from the art market applications of the market model coupled with the transaction cost data from international art auctions also suggest that the psychic returns to investing in artwork might be about 28% of the sale price. Because transaction costs are quite large in art auctions, this factor can make a substantial difference in the value of the psychic returns derived from the market model framework.

Opportunity Cost. Candela, Castellani, and Pattitoni (2013) argued that using Jensen's alpha as a way to measure psychic returns may be problematic when the assumptions of the market model do not hold. Applying an opportunity cost framework and the analytical tools of portfolio theory, they proposed a new psychic return measure, one that is not affected by the same issues as Jensen's alpha. They applied this measure of psychic return to art investments and estimated psychic returns to be in the 1%–2% range, as found when the market model has been used.

Conclusion

To some extent, psychic returns are popularity premiums—premiums paid for pleasure and enlightenment, being admired or sought after. The estimated psychic return for art investments has ranged from 1% to 2%. Transaction costs are quite large in art auctions, and this factor can make a substantial difference in the psychic returns derived from the market model framework.

3. Popularity and Asset Pricing

The risk–return paradigm continues to dominate the way in which both academicians and investment professionals think about modeling and forecasting asset prices.[22] The cause is largely the influence of the capital asset pricing model (CAPM).

The CAPM is a logical application of neoclassical economics, which also led to the efficient market hypothesis in which markets are assumed to be efficient and investors are assumed to act rationally. The key assumptions of the CAPM are that (1) market participants act rationally, (2) markets are informationally efficient, (3) investors are risk averse, and (4) investors can diversify costlessly so as to eliminate all diversifiable (nonmarket) risk. These and other assumptions lead to the conclusion that only undiversifiable risk is compensated with a premium. The CAPM produces the simple formula that the expected return is equal to the risk-free rate of return plus the security's beta (beta relative to the market) multiplied by a single premium for market risk.

After the development of the CAPM and the efficient market hypothesis, psychologists Tversky and Kahneman (1974) began to question the basic assumption that investors behave as rational agents (see also Kahneman and Tversky 1979). Behavioral finance, which Amos Tversky and Daniel Kahneman pioneered, has offered up a plethora of behavioral biases that lead to irrational behavior. Many of the biases seem to provide explanations for some of the documented ways in which observed security prices depart systematically from those that would exist in efficient markets.

Although behavioral finance tells a rich story, it has thus far not provided a full framework or theory for understanding asset prices. The CAPM and multifactor arbitrage pricing theory (APT) remain the baseline asset pricing models with which all other asset pricing models are compared.

Therefore, the analysis of investments needs a simple, coherent, and intuitive asset pricing framework for understanding and forecasting asset prices. We believe that any successful theory of asset pricing will start with the concept of popularity as we have discussed it.

In this chapter, we (1) continue to refine the popularity framework, (2) further explain the link of popularity to classical and behavioral finance, and (3) put forth a popularity-based asset pricing formula.

---

[22]As with Chapter 2, this chapter is also partially based on Ibbotson and Idzorek (2014) and Idzorek and Ibbotson (2017).

Refining the Popularity Framework

In Chapter 1, we introduced the concept of popularity, which was first presented by Ibbotson and Idzorek (2014), as an asset pricing concept that provides a unifying approach to explaining return premiums that is consistent with the risk–return framework and anomalies that are not consistent with efficient market explanations and are thus best explained by concepts in behavioral finance.

Our work started with the observation that assets represent bundles of characteristics that investors like or dislike. Conceptually, each characteristic has a supply and demand; high demand relative to supply is associated with high price, and vice versa. The price of an asset is formed by the aggregation of investor preferences. Assets with popular characteristics are expensive, and assets with unpopular characteristics are inexpensive.

The characteristics of an asset can change over time, as can investors' relative preferences. A popularity return premium goes to those who are willing to hold assets with unpopular characteristics. The premium is supplied by those willing to pay for assets with the most popular characteristics. Although individual security characteristics may migrate over time, the premiums for the unpopular characteristics themselves are relatively stable over the long term. In contrast, short-term popularity fads and distortions are interpreted here as mispricing.

The constituents of a given universe can be ranked by any characteristic or dimension of popularity—the most popular students in high school, presidential candidates, television shows, asset classes in the universe of investments, or stocks in a given market. The people/shows/asset classes/stocks with the most desirable characteristics will rank at the top, and those with undesirable characteristics will rank at the bottom. Today, reality stars and some other celebrities are famous for being famous or, in our preferred parlance, popular for being popular.

Different factors or characteristics influence popularity, but the overall popularity of the item in question can be thought of as the amalgamation of those various characteristics. Different investors make heterogeneous assessments of the benefits and costs of these characteristics, and the collective assessments result in a market-clearing price. This process relates directly to the basic principles of supply and demand: The most popular items are in short supply and high demand and, therefore, are dear.

Long-term asset pricing premiums may always be positive but can change in value. Short-term fads can lead to temporary mispricing. Finally, just as popularity is a naturally occurring behavioral phenomenon in which greater intrinsic value is attributed to popular items, so also is it natural that, within any universe for any characteristic or along any dimension of popularity, some of the most popular items will decrease in relative popularity over time while some of the least popular items will increase in relative popularity.

Precursors to the Popularity Approach

Popularity relates to a number of different bodies of literature, including efficient market equilibrium asset pricing, behavioral finance, and return premiums/anomalies. The popularity approach is most closely related to the New Equilibrium Theory (NET) put forth by Ibbotson, Diermeier, and Siegel (1984; hereafter, IDS), which we review in Chapter 4. It also relates to what is referred to as "affect" in the behavioral finance literature, with a number of behavioral biases contributing to what we call *popularity premiums.*

According to NET, assets represent bundles of characteristics in which the cost of capital (expected return) for a given asset is the aggregation of the costs of all its characteristics. NET recognizes that systematic risks (say, from the CAPM or APT) affect asset prices, as do unsystematic risks that are costly to diversify (e.g., an individual's human capital or house). NET also recognizes specific nonrisk characteristics: taxation, marketability, and information costs.

All else being equal, investors are willing to pay a premium price for an equivalent investment with a more desirable characteristic (e.g., the higher liquidity of an on-the-run US T-bond) even though it will have a lower expected return. Conversely, to hold an equivalent investment with a less desirable characteristic (e.g., the lower liquidity of real estate), investors expect a discounted price, resulting in a higher expected return.

Investors' complex assessments of the numerous characteristics of an asset or investment drive asset pricing. NET is consistent with the classical view that investors are rational, but it goes beyond both the CAPM and APT view that only systematic risks drive asset prices. *Popularity* goes beyond NET to include anomalies associated with both rationality and irrationality. Today, we believe that both systematic/nonsystematic and rational/nonrational factors form the various dimensions of popularity that drive asset pricing.

Others have approached asset pricing similarly. From the perspective of a behavioral asset pricing model, Shefrin and Statman (1994) and Anginer and Statman (2010) found that stocks with greater benefits—what we would label "popular characteristics"—have lower expected returns. Statman and Glushkov (2011) expressed a perspective similar to that of NET and popularity:

> What stocks do investors want? Many investors like large-cap stocks, growth stocks and, perhaps, stocks of "socially responsible" companies, such as those with good employee relations. Stocks with greater benefits fetch higher prices, and higher prices correspond to lower expected returns. (p. 5)

33

Surprisingly, in a 2016 interview, Eugene Fama, who was awarded the Nobel Prize in economics for developing the efficient market hypothesis, said the following:

> Value stocks tend to be companies that have few investment opportunities and aren't very profitable. Maybe people just don't like that type of company. That to me has more appeal than a mispricing story, because mispricing, at least in the standard economic framework, should eventually correct itself, whereas taste can go on forever. (Fama and Thaler 2016)

Popularity is an intuitive and naturally occurring behavioral phenomenon associated with being admired, sought after, well-known, and/or accepted. It is observed in countless settings. From a behavioral literature perspective, the idea of popularity is closely linked to *affect*, which Statman, Fisher, and Anginer (2008) described as the specific quality of goodness or badness. Affect, or *sentiment*, is closely linked to the intuitive concept of popularity in that it describes emotional or automatic *feelings* regarding an asset, investment, or company and the way those emotions influence cognitive decision making. Zajonc (1980) concluded that affect may have a stronger influence on decision making than do cognitive processes, with affect and cognitive processes under the control of partially independent systems.[23]

Popularity goes somewhat beyond behavioral finance in that it explicitly accounts for rational preferences that may or may not be influenced by emotions. Specifically, affect focuses on emotional reactions and seems to exclude observable anomalies that are the result of rational preferences, such as greater liquidity or preferential tax treatment. Affect seems like a good *contributor* to popularity. Statman, Fisher, and Anginer (2008) and Anginer and Statman (2010) incorporated affect into a behavioral asset pricing model. But even without the affect heuristic, rational popularity premiums that are consistent with NET would still exist.

Efficient Markets, Behavioral Finance, or Something Else?

In Chapter 1, we explained how popularity straddles classical and behavioral finance. We believe that popularity can be consistent with both camps; thus, it can be thought of as a unifying asset pricing theory. The formalization of the

---

[23]Attempting to assess and value important characteristics is not just a human psychological phenomenon; it is an innate activity required for survival that goes hand in hand with Charles Darwin's ideas about natural selection. Just as strength or size may have assisted in Darwinian survival, investor security selection of various traits can increase or decrease wealth, but as imperfect humans, we make mistakes (which are somewhat self-correcting from both a Darwinian and an investor perspective).

theory of popularity moves beyond the paradigm that more return requires more risk (e.g., CAPM or APT) to an enriched framework in which relative popularity drives returns.

From an efficient market perspective, one can take the view not only that the market is efficient at pricing risk but also that a number of other characteristics are being priced by investors with their heterogeneous attitudes toward those characteristics, as expressed in NET. Since popularity is a social phenomenon, the popularity approach seems to emerge from the behavioral finance perspective. Investors fail to make nearly instantaneously rational decisions for a variety of reasons: affect, lack of attention, loss aversion, overconfidence, anchoring, mental accounting, and so on. For example, investors who are overly confident may go after the most popular stocks and end up driving the price way up. If these biases are only temporarily connected with a security, they result in mispricing; however, more-permanent biases related to groups of securities can result in long-term premiums (e.g., the value effect). In both the classical and behavioral interpretations of popularity, in the long run, the winners hold the unpopular stocks and those who hold popular stocks are willing or unknowing losers.

The main idea of the efficient market hypothesis is that all *relevant* information about the value of securities is reflected in the market prices of securities. Hence, the market price of each security is "fair" and reflects its "intrinsic value." This makes active management futile. However, if the market is inefficient, not all relevant information is reflected in market prices. Hence, some securities are underpriced and some are overpriced relative to their unknown fair values. If prices tend toward fair values, active management can succeed if active managers can estimate fair values with some accuracy.

Popularity theory suggests that the efficient-versus-inefficient, dichotomous view of market efficiency is inadequate. The failure of all relevant information to be reflected in market prices is not the only manner in which prices may not be fair. Prices may also reflect *irrelevant* information, such as the behavioral preferences of investors. In such a case, rather than being inefficient in the usual sense, the market can be said to be "beyond efficient."[24] In an efficient market, prices are fair, but in a market that is beyond efficient, prices are "biased" because of investor preferences. To be precise, a biased security price is a price that reflects both relevant and irrelevant information in a beyond-efficient market. The bias in the price of a security is the percentage difference between the price of the security in a beyond-efficient market

---

[24]In saying a market is "beyond efficient," we are not saying that it is better than an efficient market but, rather, that it embeds both relevant and irrelevant information in security prices.

and its price in an efficient market. The bias could be positive or negative. In Chapter 5, we present a formal model of a market that is beyond efficient with such biased prices.

Figure 3.1 presents a complex Venn diagram to illustrate the interaction and subcomponents of the neoclassical and behavioral economics camps in the context of popularity. The left side represents the neoclassical economic view and illustrates the intersection between the CAPM and NET, both of which are nested under the classical view of the world. The CAPM and NET assume that investors are rational, but NET allows for additional characteristics to influence asset prices in a rational manner.

The right side of Figure 3.1 represents the behavioral finance view, for which we have identified a potpourri of potential behaviors afflicting real-world investors. Representing behavioral finance in this kind of diagram is, arguably, more challenging than representing classical finance because the behavioral area is a bit of a catch-all for a variety of observed behaviors and potential explanations. The largest behavioral theory that can be used to explain a number of the observable so-called irrational investor behaviors is *prospect theory*. Prospect theory posits diminishing increases in joy for increasingly better outcomes and rising increases in pain for increasingly dire outcomes, particularly related to one's current endowment. Prospect theory is related to framing, anchoring, and the endowment effect.

Figure 3.1. Venn Diagram of Neoclassical Economics, Behavioral Economics, and Popularity

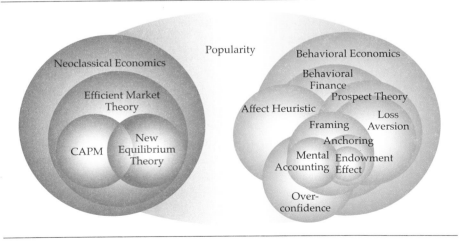

Source: Based on Exhibit 2 in Idzorek and Ibbotson (2017).

Figure 3.2.   Major Asset Pricing Theories

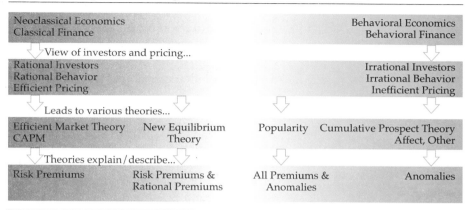

Source: Based on Exhibit 3 in Idzorek and Ibbotson (2017).

Mostly contained within behavioral finance and somewhat intersecting with prospect theory is the affect heuristic. As explained earlier, the notion of affect is similar to popularity and involves emotional decisions that either override or bias rational, cognitive decisions. Affect helps explain irrational popularity premiums but not rational, non-risk-oriented premiums (e.g., liquidity). As illustrated in Figure 3.1, popularity intersects with the majority of both camps: Risk in a CAPM sense is unpopular; the rationally unpopular premiums of NET are rewarded, and affect-based premiums align with popularity, as do the other premiums explained by prospect theory.

Through a different lens, **Figure 3.2** identifies the contrasting perceptions of the investor (a purely rational person versus an everyday real person) and the spectrum that this creates. Each particular view of the investor leads to one of the various asset pricing theories: CAPM, NET, popularity, affect, and prospect theory. Of these, the CAPM is perfectly suited for a formulaic view of asset prices, whereas prospect theory is the least suited to a formulaic view of asset prices.

A Popularity-Based Asset Pricing Formula

We suspect that many of the factors we have discussed are *priced factors* that can be considered premiums in a pricing equation.[25] We consider these to

---

[25]We introduce the popularity-based asset pricing formula in this section, but Chapter 5 presents a more rigorous development of the suggested pricing formula.

be dimensions of popularity that are systematically unpopular over an extended period.

The concept of popularity tells us the direction of the popularity premiums but, thus far, has not provided us with a precise toolkit for estimating their magnitude. In **Figure 3.3**, we start to outline a potential linear asset pricing formula based on popularity that simultaneously considers both rational and irrational asset pricing factors.

At the top of Figure 3.3, we have somewhat loosely identified traditional and potential popularity-based factors and ordered them from rational to irrational. On the one hand, market risk, size, value, liquidity, and severe downside risk are factors a rational investor would price because they are all characteristics that an investor would seek or want to avoid. On the other hand, competitive sustainable advantage, brand power, and company reputation should already be baked into the price in a rationally efficient market and, therefore, should not be important to a rational investor who only cares about risk and return. For simplicity, tractability, and comparability, we present a linear pricing formula with limited factors.

Beginning with the CAPM formula, the pricing models are listed down the side. In this way, the connection of the popularity model with the other asset pricing formulas is illustrated—from the CAPM to versions of the Fama–French multifactor model (Fama and French 1996), to a linear formula based on NET, and finally to a potentially fully specified popularity-based asset pricing formula that includes momentum (Carhart 1997). This final formula starts with the CAPM, and then, factors are added and adjustments made for additional rational and irrational pricing factors based on the various dimensions of popularity.

We see this build-up as in the spirit of the linear equation of the APT (Ross 1976), the Fama–French extension of the CAPM, NET of IDS, and the behavioral asset pricing model of Statman and Glushkov (2011).[26]

The popularity asset pricing formula depicted in Figure 3.3 is not complete and lacks a rigorous derivation. Chapter 5 presents a formal and rigorously derived PAPM (popularity asset pricing model) that may contain any number of popularity premiums, each multiplied by a security-specific

---

[26]Statman and Glushkov (2011) developed a six-factor model consisting of the Fama–French–Carhart factors plus two socially responsible factors: (1) top minus bottom, which is the difference between the returns of stocks of companies ranked high and low according to such criteria as employee relations and environmental responsibility, and (2) accepted minus shunned, which is the difference between the returns of stocks commonly accepted by socially responsible investors and of stocks commonly shunned by them, such as stocks of producers of tobacco and weapons.

Figure 3.3. Toward a Popularity-Based Asset Pricing Formula

	Rational								Irrational
	Risk-Free Rate	Market (MKT)	Size (SMB)	Value (HML)	Liquidity (LIQ)	Risk Anomalies (RISKA)	Environmental, Social, Governance (ESG)	Competitive Advantage, Brand, Reputation (CABR)	Momentum (MOM)
CAPM	$E[R_i] = R_f + B_{i1}E[R_{MKT} - R_f]$								
Fama–French 3-Factor	$E[R_i] = R_f + B_{i1}E[R_{MKT} - R_f] + B_{i2}SMB + B_{i3}HML$								
NET*	$E[R_i] = R_f + B_{i1}E[R_{MKT} - R_f] + B_{i2}SMB + B_{i3}HML + B_{i4}LIQ + B_{i5}RISKA$								
Popularity**	$E[R_i] = R_f + B_{i1}E[R_{MKT} - R_f] + B_{i2}SMB + B_{i3}HML + B_{i4}LIQ + B_{i5}RISKA + B_{i6}ESG + B_{i7}CABR + B_{i8}MOM$								

Note: SMB stands for small minus big (the size factor); HML stands for high book/market minus low book/market (the value factor).

*NET does not specify an asset pricing formula, nor does it identify an exact list of "rational" factors; thus, this formula represents a potential specification of a linear asset pricing formula.

**The popularity asset pricing formula captures a subset of the characteristics that form the various dimensions of popularity.

Source: Based on Exhibit 4 in Idzorek and Ibbotson (2017).

loading. These popularity loadings are based on intrinsic characteristics of securities that investors either like or dislike. Hence, they are not directly linked to the market-based variables used to measure the size, value, risk anomalies, and momentum factor loadings in Figure 3.3. We regard these market-based variables as proxies for underlying popularity loadings.[27]

Statman and Glushkov (2011) argued that in classical finance, the factors in a Fama–French model are interpreted as risk, whereas from a behavioral view, the factors are "interpreted as reflections of the expressive and emotional benefits of positive affect" (p. 6). From a popularity perspective, the factors reflect preferences regarding a collection of characteristics that investors like or dislike, in which some of the preferences are rational and others are irrational. Although these factors are commonly thought of as risk factors, the use of the word "risk" is misleading because exposure to many of the factors (valuation, liquidity, etc.) does not necessarily entail more risk.

An important question is why the various popularity premiums seem to be permanent, even after they have been discovered and could potentially be exploited and eliminated. Given the recent rapid increase in the popularity of so-called smart-beta and factor-based investment approaches designed to capitalize on what we call popularity premiums, we expect that some of these premiums will eventually diminish. Some may even reverse as the historically popular becomes unpopular and the historically unpopular becomes popular. Candidates for reversal include low-volatility strategies, which appear to be increasing in popularity. The liquidity premium, however, is unlikely to experience an actual reversal because investors will always prefer more liquidity to less. A more likely outcome could be a reduction in the magnitude of the liquidity premium.

---

[27]The equations in Figure 3.3 may be interpreted in two ways. The first way is to interpret the factor loadings (B_{i2}, B_{i3}, and so on) as coefficients derived from security characteristics (both intrinsic and market based) and interpret *SMB*, *HML*, and so on, as factor premiums. For example, the factor loading for size, B_{i2}, could be based on the logarithm of security i's market capitalization and SMB is the size premium. This is the interpretation that we use in the text. The alternative interpretation is to view the equations in Figure 3.3 as being derived from time-series regressions, as in Fama and French (1993). In this interpretation, the factor loadings are the coefficients from a time-series regression of the security's excess returns on the excess returns on the market portfolio (B_{i1}) and other various time series (B_{i2}, B_{i3}, etc.), such as Fama and French's SMB and HML time-series factors, which themselves are derived from time series of returns on indexes. In this interpretation, *SMB*, *HML*, and so on in Figure 3.3 are the expected values of time-series factors that bear their names.

Popularity and Speculative Bubbles

Similar to our explanation or rationale for how changes in relative popularity can be used to explain price momentum, we believe popularity can help explain bubbles. Let us consider the two most recent examples of so-called irrational exuberance—the technology bubble of the late 1990s and the housing bubble associated with the 2008 financial crisis.[28] Both episodes might be characterized as investing fads that affected large segments of the market rather than a single company. In the 1990s, a point was reached in which it seemed everyone was talking about how much money they were making with internet stocks. Investment clubs were a fad. Similarly, in the years prior to 2008, people were purchasing multiple homes with little to no money down.

One might think of these two bubbles as following the classic price momentum pattern. In both cases, some sort of catalyst began to draw increased investor attention to a sector. Because of arbitrage shorting limits, that new-found attention led to an increase in net demand, which simultaneously increased turnover (trading activity). The increase in demand resulted in abnormal price increases, which in turn, resulted in more attention and more demand. A virtuous circle took hold. Eventually, popularity peaked. And as the price exceeded the justifiable price based on fundamentals by ever increasing amounts, attracting enough new fools to maintain the prices became impossible. The tipping point was reached, and the virtuous circle was replaced with a vicious circle as popularity, demand, price, and realized returns all plummeted.

Others have observed and documented this type of pattern. For example, Hong and Stein (2007) charted the corresponding increase in share turnover and internet stock prices followed by the subsequent decrease in share turnover and internet stock prices associated with the dot-com stock bubble between 1997 and 2002. They noted similar volume-linked patterns associated with the 1720 South Sea Bubble (Bank of England stock) and the US stock market crash in the late 1920s.

---

[28]Although on a smaller scale than the others, the exuberance around all things Bitcoin might be an even more recent example.

Conclusion

In this chapter, we continued to develop the popularity framework and laid the groundwork for a popularity-based equilibrium asset pricing theory that would explain almost all of the well-known premiums and anomalies. Many of the cases of mispricing seem also to be consistent with the popularity concept.

Popularity treats securities as bundles of characteristics, some of which are nearly universally liked or disliked by investors, resulting in priced characteristics that we think of as various dimensions of popularity. Although risk is the most important priced characteristic, investors have preferences for a number of other characteristics that may or may not result in more risk. Popularity applies to all priced characteristics—those that seem rational and those that seem irrational. Popularity builds on NET and is closely related to the affect heuristic of behavioral finance. A number of the behavioral biases associated with behavioral finance contribute to the concept of popularity and popularity premiums.

A popularity-based asset pricing theory can be advanced either from a classical efficient market view, in which one assumes the market is efficient at pricing the rational dimensions of popularity, or from an irrational view. In both interpretations of popularity, the winners hold the unpopular stocks (or other securities) and those who hold popular stocks are willing or unknowing losers.

Finally, we put forth a potential popularity-based multifactor linear asset pricing formula in which the expected return of an asset is related to a variety of exposures to the various dimensions of popularity. In the next two chapters, we show how such a formula can be derived in a formal equilibrium model.

4. New Equilibrium Theory

In 1984, Ibbotson, Diermeier, and Siegel (hereafter, IDS) published an article in the *Financial Analysts Journal* that was a precursor to the popularity framework. They dubbed their framework "New Equilibrium Theory" (NET). In this chapter, we review NET, largely by quoting IDS.

NET was presented in the classical framework but expanded beyond risk preferences to include market frictions. Popularity extends the demand preferences to include both classical and behavioral preferences. The ideas, however, are similar—namely, that preferences, whatever the source, are priced.

IDS lacked a formal economic model and used charts with informal supply and demand curves. A major advance in this book is that we have developed a formal economic model, which we present fully in the next chapter, that embodies their ideas. Here, we introduce part of that model so that we can present IDS's central ideas mathematically instead of using their supply and demand graphical analysis.

The Central Ideas of NET

IDS summarized their ideas in the abstract of their article:

Investors demand more of an asset, the more desirable the asset's characteristics. The most important characteristic is its price, or expected return. By varying price, any and all assets become desirable enough for the capital market to clear.

Asset characteristics other than price include both risk and non-risk characteristics. The Capital Asset Pricing Model and Arbitrage Pricing Theory [APT] have described the risk characteristics. The non-risk characteristics are not as well understood. They include taxation, marketability and information costs. For many assets, these non-risk characteristics affect price, or expected return, even more than the risk characteristics.

Investors regard asset characteristics as positive or negative costs, and investors evaluate expected returns net of these costs. The New Equilibrium Theory (NET) framework applies to all assets—including stocks and bonds, real estate, venture capital, durables, and intangibles such as human capital—and incorporates all asset characteristics. (p. 22)

Note that the costs that IDS explicitly mention—taxation, marketability, and information costs—all fall under the heading of *frictional*, which is a subset of *classical* characteristics in the taxonomy of characteristics that we presented in Chapter 1. In other words, NET is an attempt to expand the classical framework to take into account security characteristics that a rational investor would consider but that are assumed away in such classical models as the CAPM and APT. As we shall do in the next chapter, the main idea of NET can easily be expanded to include the *behavioral* characteristics included in our taxonomy in Chapter 1.

IDS started their article as follows:

> Prices in capital markets are set by the interaction of demand and supply. This relationship is commonly expressed in terms of the "supply of and demand for capital." But viewing it from the opposite perspective—that is, in terms of the demand for and supply of capital market *returns*—has the advantage of focusing our attention on returns as the goods being priced in the marketplace. This article provides a framework for analyzing the demand for capital market returns, which we define as the compensation each investor requires for holding assets with various characteristics. (p. 22) [Emphasis in original.]

The authors continued as follows:

> The basics of the demand for capital market returns can be explained in a few sentences. Investors regard each asset as a bundle of characteristics for which they have various preferences and aversions. Investors translate each characteristic into a cost and require compensation in the form of expected returns for bearing these costs. Thus, although all investors are assumed to perceive the same before-cost expected return for any given asset, each has individually determined costs he must pay to hold that asset. On the basis of perceived expected returns net of these individually determined costs, investors choose to hold differing amounts of each asset. The cost of capital for an asset is the aggregation of all investors' capital costs on the margin and represents the market expected return on the asset. (p. 22)

The authors then went on to contrast NET with existing theories:

> Formal demand-side theories such as the Capital Asset Pricing Model (CAPM) and Arbitrage Pricing Theory (APT) have prescribed useful mathematical formulations for deriving assets' expected returns. Both these theories, however, assume perfect capital markets in which all costs are due specifically to risk. The CAPM specifies the payoff demanded by investors for bearing one cost—beta, or market, risk; APT treats multiple risk factors. Other research has addressed non-risk factors but in isolation. (pp. 22–23)

They concluded their opening as follows:

> Our framework, which we term New Equilibrium Theory (NET), inte-grates costs arising from all sources—including various risks, as well as

taxability, marketability, and information costs—and affecting all assets in an investor's opportunity set—stocks, bonds, real estate, human capital, venture capital, tangibles, and intangibles. NET theory does not provide a detailed analysis of each particular cost, nor does it specify a mathematical asset pricing equation. The NET model is useful, however, in explaining observed investor behavior. (p. 23)

IDS presented NET in a supply-and-demand graphical analysis, wherein supply is relatively fixed and demand is aggregated across investors. The demand curves reflect investor preferences for more liquidity, less taxation, and so on. Because each investor is risk averse, the marginal demand from each investor is downward sloping for each security or asset class. Consequently, each investor holds a diversified portfolio, not loading up on any one security or asset class.

In the next chapter, we present a formal model that embodies the main idea of NET, part of which we present here. From this model, we derive the mathematical asset pricing equation that NET lacked.

A Formal Model for NET

IDS expressed the main ideas of NET as follows:

> The objective of the NET framework is to determine the equilibrium cost of capital, r_j, for each asset j in the market, given the characteristics of asset j and the utility functions of all the investors in the market. Conceptually, the cost of capital is the sum of all capital costs *at the margin* across all holders of all claims on asset j; it is typically expressed as a per year percentage of value. This cost of capital can also be interpreted as an expected return to investors or as a discount rate used in valuation. (p. 23) [Emphasis added.]

They continued to develop the model as follows:

> To focus on the composite market's cost of capital for asset j, we assume [the first key assumption] that investors have homogeneous expectations concerning r_j, the asset's expected return before investors' costs, as well as r_f, the rate of return on the characteristic-free [i.e., risk-free] asset. Our second key assumption is that investors have heterogeneous, or individually determined, costs associated with the holding of asset j. These differing costs are a natural consequence of the fact that investors differ in regard to wealth, risk aversion, access to information, tax bracket, and numerous other traits. The individual investor may evaluate an asset's characteristics according to his own classification scheme, and he may measure an asset's characteristics according to his own judgment. Thus, each investor will have his own particular utility function, according to which he translates all asset characteristics, including all risks, into [marginal] costs. (pp. 23–24)

To state these ideas formally, we extend the mean–variance utility function to include security characteristics besides risk and expected return.

Let:

n = the number of risky securities in the market
$\vec{\mu}$ = the n-element vector of expected excess returns (in excess of r_f)
Ψ = the $n \times n$ variance–covariance matrix of returns on the risky securities
$\vec{x}_i$ = the n-element vector of investor i's allocations to the risky securities[29]
λ_i = the risk aversion parameter of investor i
p = the number of characteristics (besides risk and expected excess return)
$\mathbf{C}$ = $n \times p$ matrix of characteristics of the securities
$\vec{\varphi}_i$ = p-element vector of investor i's attitudes toward the characteristics

Note that in the NET model, the elements of $\vec{\varphi}_i$ are usually negative, reflecting various degrees of dislike, but can be positive. By allowing for positive values, this model can be generalized to include characteristics that investors like—that is, popular characteristics.

For clarity, we start with the mean–variance utility-maximization problem for investor i:

$$\max_{\vec{x}_i} U_i(\vec{x}_i) = \vec{\mu}'\vec{x}_i - \frac{\lambda_i}{2}\vec{x}_i'\Psi\vec{x}_i. \tag{4.1}$$

Investor i's problem is to maximize $U_i(\vec{x}_i)$ by his or her choice of $\vec{x}_i$—that is, through portfolio selection.

The utility function in Equation 4.1 contains a benefit $(\vec{\mu}'\vec{x}_i)$ and a penalty $[(\lambda_i/2)\vec{x}_i'\Psi\vec{x}_i]$. One might extend this utility function to account for additional attitudes toward characteristics in various ways: as an adjustment or new term representing the benefit or as an adjustment or new term for the penalty. Here, we choose to include a new term that adds to (or subtracts from) the total benefit:

$$\max_{\vec{x}_i} U_i(\vec{x}_i) = \vec{\mu}'\vec{x}_i + \vec{\varphi}'\mathbf{C}'\vec{x}_i - \frac{\lambda_i}{2}\vec{x}_i'\Psi\vec{x}_i. \tag{4.2}$$

From the first-order condition of this problem, we have

$$\vec{\mu} = \lambda_i\Psi\vec{x}_i - \mathbf{C}\vec{\varphi}_i. \tag{4.3}$$

---

[29]The investor allocates $1 - \sum_{j=1}^{n} x_{ij}$ to the risk-free security.

We can interpret this condition in terms of IDS's ideas. The right-hand side of Equation 4.3 shows how "each investor will have his own particular utility function, according to which he translates all asset characteristics, including all risks, into [marginal] costs" (p. 24). The marginal risk costs are given by $\lambda_i \Psi \bar{x}$, and the marginal nonrisk costs are given by $-C\vec{\varphi}_i$. The sum of these two terms is investor i's demand for capital market returns. The left-hand side of Equation 4.3 is the supply of excess capital market returns and is not specific to any individual. The investor holds the portfolio that equates the demand for capital market returns to the supply of capital market returns. In the next chapter, we show how aggregating this condition across investors leads to an asset pricing formula that includes market risk and nonrisk characteristics that could be frictional or behavioral, thus fulfilling the objective of NET and going beyond it.

Issues That the NET Framework Can Address

IDS discussed a number of issues that the NET framework can address. In the following subsections, we quote them on specific issues.

Financial Intermediation.

The NET framework can readily be expanded to include repackaging opportunities on the part of issuing firms or financial intermediaries. The role of the financial intermediary is to repackage the pricing characteristics so as to reduce investor costs. One way intermediaries accomplish their task is by making the markets for pricing characteristics more complete. By unbundling asset characteristics, for example, they increase the likelihood that those investors with lower costs for a particular characteristic will hold that characteristic in their portfolios. Another way intermediaries reduce investor costs is by optimal bundling of asset characteristics to take advantage of economies of scale.

Investors perceive financial intermediaries as additional asset offerings, whereas issuers perceive them [the intermediaries] as additional investors. Assuming perfect competition, intermediaries act to maximize aggregate investor surplus by minimizing the sum of *all* investor costs . . . across all assets for all the pricing characteristics. (pp. 26–27) [Emphasis in original.]

Risk Characteristics. IDS described the various risks covered in their approach thus:

The CAPM states that only one risk-pricing characteristic exists—namely, market risk. APT provides for multiple risk-pricing characteristics, and treats each risk as orthogonal to all of the others, so that the market payoffs

47

are additive. The NET framework does not directly take sides in this controversy but does allow for multiple pricing characteristics. We focus here on four of the most intuitive types of risk—beta (market), inflation, real interest rate, and residual risk.

Market, or beta, risk is the risk that the return of an asset will fluctuate with the market portfolio's return. According to CAPM, beta risk is the only risk that affects expected return. It is assumed that the rational investor will diversify away (at no cost) all other risks. In the NET framework, as noted, each investor translates risks into costs by assigning a price at which he is indifferent between buying and not buying more of the risk.

Inflation risk is the risk that an asset's real value will fluctuate because of unanticipated changes in the inflation rate. This risk is best exemplified by a long-term government bond, which is relatively free of most other pricing characteristics. The bond is a nominal contract, and its yield to maturity consists of three components—the expected inflation rate, the expected real interest rate, and the risk premium (if any) associated with inflation and real interest rates. Although the market anticipates all three components over the bond's life, unanticipated changes in current and expected inflation rates cause variations in the bond's real return.

Inflation risk arises when one side explicitly or implicitly contracts in nominal, instead of real, terms. For this pricing characteristic to be nonzero, at least one side must have negative inflation risk costs and be willing to pay the other side to create these risks. The inflation risk premium may be positive for investors in the stock market and for holders of short-term, and possibly long-term, bonds. Other assets likely to contain a nonzero amount of inflation risk include real estate, gold, and any other assets whose real returns are correlated (positively or negatively) with unanticipated changes in the inflation rate. (pp. 27–28)

The authors went on to put real interest rate risk into the NET context:

The real interest rate is the difference between the instantaneous nominal interest rate (on a characteristic-free bond) and the instantaneous inflation rate. Since real interest rate changes are unanticipated, the investor who rolls over a series of short-term bonds receives an uncertain return in real terms. The investor in long-term bonds can lock in the real rate over the bond's life but incurs inflation risk in the process. It is, of course, possible to construct a long-term contract in real terms [TIPS are such contracts.[30]] and avoid both inflation and real interest rate risk for any given time horizon. (pp. 28–29)

---

[30]Treasury Inflation-Protected Securities are examples of long-term contracts in real terms.

They then described residual risk in the NET context:

Residual risk is the risk resulting from lack of diversification in a portfolio. Assuming that the risks already described account for an asset's undiversifiable risk, residual risk is the one remaining risk factor. We propose that residual risk, like the other risk factors, may be an *ex ante* pricing factor.

In CAPM, the rational investor perfectly diversifies so as to eliminate entirely all residual risk. NET assumes that it is costly to diversify. The factors that make perfect diversification either impossible or suboptimal are related to non-risk pricing characteristics. For example, many investors wish to own their residences outright. The large unit size of other real estate investments, along with the high cost of creating divisibility mechanisms such as condominiums and limited partnerships, imposes high costs on investors seeking diversification. Thus, most investors do not hold a diversified real estate portfolio—that is, one that is spread over various geographical locations and types of land and structures. (p. 29)

The authors concluded their litany of risks by addressing human capital:

Human capital is subject to even more extreme constraints on diversification. Once acquired, human capital cannot readily be sold and is usually rented out for wages in the labor market. It follows that one cannot easily buy a portion of another person's human capital in order to diversify within the asset class. (p. 29)

Idiosyncratic risk is usually uncompensated in asset pricing theory. But some investments may be difficult to diversify, such as an owner-occupied house or human capital. In such cases, idiosyncratic risk itself may merit a risk premium. We focus on stocks in this book, but even in the pure equity case, an entrepreneur's concentrated position may have its value reduced by the entrepreneur's need to consider the total risk, rather than simply the beta risk, of his or her investment. Closely held companies may also be illiquid. This combination may lower valuations considerably, leading to high but volatile expected returns that are hard to realize.

Taxability. IDS then addressed nonrisk costs, one example of which is taxes:

Taxability often has a substantial impact on an asset's cost of capital. The taxability characteristic is inherently complex because of the intricacies of the U.S. (and other countries') taxation systems. This complexity consists of (1) the stepwise ("tax bracket") and multiplicative attributes of the tax function; (2) the fact that taxes on a given asset are contingent on the performance (effect on income) of other assets in one's portfolio; (3) the differential treatment of ordinary income and capital gains; (4) special tax laws, such as those allowing depreciation much faster than the useful life of certain assets; and (5) multiple taxing authorities. These attributes cause the tax costs for the same asset to differ across individuals. The general principle is that highly taxable assets are lower priced—i.e., have a higher before-tax expected return—than less highly taxed assets.

For example, municipal bonds, whose coupons are free of U.S. federal income taxes, yield 20 to 50 percent less than fully taxable corporate bonds of comparable risk. A similar relationship has been suggested for high dividend versus low dividend stocks. Constantinides [1983] provides a personal tax equilibrium that includes the timing option for the realization of capital losses and the deferral of capital gains. Most of these and other tax-related theoretical results can be introduced into the general NET framework because NET does not specify actual investor costs.

Real estate, venture capital, hedging portfolios, and leasing arrangements provide special opportunities for financial intermediaries to separate out tax characteristics and repackage them for the appropriate clienteles. After repackaging, many investments may be tax shelters having negative tax rates.

In summary, an asset may generate taxes (positive or negative) on income, expenses, or capital appreciation. The investor includes these tax costs in his pricing process. The complexity of the taxation system and the interaction of taxes with other pricing characteristics make it difficult to specify this pricing characteristic. Nevertheless, the magnitude of taxes is sufficiently large that it must be included in any exposition of the NET framework. (p. 29)

Marketability, Information, Search, Transaction, and Divisibility Costs.
Marketability costs, referred to in more modern language as "illiquidity" or the cost to achieve liquidity, are another nonrisk cost:

We group all the entry and exit costs associated with buying or selling an asset into the category of marketability costs. The NET framework . . . provides no description of how an investor came to hold his particular portfolio or when or how he may rebalance his portfolio. For the NET equilibrium to be descriptive, each investor must reduce the value of his assets by a present value amount to cover these costs. These marketability costs include information, search and transaction, and divisibility costs. (pp. 29–30)

Information costs, search and transaction costs, and divisibility costs each have their own unique attributes:

Information costs are the costs that an investor must pay to learn the value of an asset. Since the NET model assumes homogeneous expectations, we have already in some sense assumed these costs away. Nevertheless, we can informally apply the NET model by suggesting that investors must pay some costs to learn what the homogeneous expectations are. In such a world, investors with comparatively lower information costs for a particular asset would tend to own that asset. For example, U.S. investors own stocks and bonds of U.S. corporations in disproportionately large quantities because of the cost of acquiring information across national boundaries. Moreover, assets that are difficult to learn about, such as stocks of small or new companies, should have higher before-cost expected returns than assets that are easier to learn about, such as large-company stocks. Finally, information costs tend to favor the large investor, since there are economies of scale in information use.

Search and transaction costs include the costs of looking for the other side of the transaction, as well as the costs of actually closing the transaction. The costs may include the bid–ask spread, the waiting time beyond the investor's desired horizon, the possibility of having to take a price concession, the paperwork and legal costs accompanying a transaction, the cost of advertising or other efforts to locate the other party to the transaction, and the cost of any brokers or agents used to effect the transaction. These costs are treated in search and bargaining theory literature. In the NET framework, these costs are merely estimated by the investor as their present value equivalent costs.

Divisibility costs arise from the large and discrete scale of some investments, such as real estate, venture capital, large-denomination certificates of indebtedness, and certain discrete human capital decisions. Divisibility interacts with many of the other pricing characteristics. Indivisibility's chief burden to investors may be that it forces them to take substantial residual risk. It also causes some investors to hold a suboptimal quantity of a particular investment. (p. 30)

Human capital, the authors write, can be treated like any other asset, but with its own unique characteristics:

Human capital, once acquired, is often considered nonmarketable as well as indivisible. It can be rented and, to some extent, it can be put up as collateral for loans. When invested in a business, portions of it can sometimes be sold. In the NET framework, we can regard these as high, but not insurmountable, divisibility costs. In some models, an equilibrium is arrived at in which human capital is literally treated as non-marketable. (p. 30)

In many settings, divisibility costs can be overcome:

One of the principal roles of financial intermediaries is to repackage securities in such a way as to reduce divisibility costs. A saver (small lender) would have great difficulty in finding a borrower with whom to transact and still maintain the liquidity of his savings. By pooling the savings of many persons, a bank can do exactly that. Money market funds reduce the minimum investment amount for cash instruments from $10,000 to very little. Real estate investment trusts and limited partnerships lower the size barrier for investing in large properties from the range of millions of dollars to the range of thousands or less. Each of these mechanisms for reducing divisibility costs is itself costly. For many investors, however, paying the costs of investing through a financial intermediary increases their investor surplus. (p. 30)

The authors conclude by listing other possible pricing factors:

Other miscellaneous factors may affect the price of a capital market asset. These include nonpecuniary costs or benefits, all of which we would treat as positive or negative costs. In addition, certain expenses, such as management, maintenance, and storage costs, are best treated as costs of capital rather than as decrements to cash flow. This is because they differ across investors. Because investors seek to maximize returns net of all costs and benefits, these factors should be included in the set of NET pricing factors. (p. 30)

Note the connection to our present work, which regards nonpecuniary costs and benefits as critical to asset pricing.

Asset Class Characteristics

IDS included a table of the characteristics of various asset classes that should be priced in the NET framework. We provide this table here as **Exhibit 4.1**. These characteristics are classified according to being related to risks, taxability, and marketability as discussed in the preceding quotations.

Conclusion

NET is a classical precursor to the popularity asset pricing model because it is based on a principle for understanding how investors' attitudes toward the nonrisk characteristics of securities affect how securities are priced in an equilibrium model. NET can easily be extended to include behavioral preferences, as we do in this book.

Although the creators of the NET framework, Ibbotson, Diermeier, and Siegel (1984), did not develop a formal equilibrium model, they had a number of insights related to the costs of owning securities that rational investors would consider when making investment decisions. In this chapter,

Exhibit 4.1. Asset Class Characteristics Priced in NET

Asset	Risks					Marketability			Miscellaneous Factors
	Stock Market Beta	Inflation	Real Interest Rate	Residual Risk Cost[a]	Taxability[a]	Information Costs[a]	Search & Transaction Costs	Divisibility Costs	
Large-company stocks	Near one	Low positive	Positive?	Near zero	Low	Low	Low	Very low	Probably efficiently priced
Small-company stocks	Varies	Low positive	Positive?	Low	Low	High	Medium[a]	Very low	
T-bonds	Near zero	Positive	Low	Near zero	High	Low	Low	Medium[a]	Efficiently priced
Corporate bonds	Low	Positive	Low	Near zero	High	Low	Low	Medium[a]	
Municipal bonds	Near zero	Positive	Low	Low	Zero	Low	Low	Medium[a]	
T-bills	Zero	Zero	High	Near zero	High	Low	Low	High[a]	
Houses, condos	Low	?	?	High	Negative	High	High[a]	Very high[a]	High management costs
Gold	Zero or negative	Negative?	?	Low	Low	Low	Low	Very low	No income; portable
Art	Low	Negative?	?	High	Low	Very high	Very high	Very high	Nonpecuniary benefits; no income
Foreign securities	Varies	Varies	?	Varies	Low	High	Varies	Low	
Human capital	High	?	?	Very high	Very high	High	High[a]	Very high[a]	Cannot sell, only rent or borrow against

[a]Financial intermediaries are likely to be important in reducing these costs.
Source: IDS.

we showed how such costs can be incorporated into an investor utility function and how the first-order condition for maximizing that utility function matches the authors' notion of equating the supply of and the demand for capital market returns. In the next chapter, this first-order condition is the starting point for a formal equilibrium model in which investors' attitudes toward all characteristics, both rational and irrational, determine asset prices.

5. The Popularity Asset Pricing Model

The capital asset pricing model (CAPM) has been the dominant model of expected returns for more than 50 years. Chapter 2 noted that, despite the distinction of the theory, subsequent empirical research has established the existence of various premiums and anomalies that violate the CAPM. Perhaps the model's biggest strength—expressing investor preferences solely in terms of risk—is also its biggest limitation. Investors care about many characteristics having little to do with risk that we consider to be dimensions of *popularity*. These features include such asset characteristics as liquidity, taxability, scalability, divisibility, controllability, transparency, and the components of sustainability—namely, environmental, social, and governance (ESG) factors.

This chapter addresses nonrisk characteristics in a CAPM-like framework based on the concept of popularity that we discussed in Chapters 1–3 with an equilibrium model that we call the "popularity asset pricing model" (PAPM). In Chapter 3, we introduced the concept of a market that is "beyond efficient," in which information irrelevant to "fair" value is reflected in security prices as a result of investors' behavioral preferences. In such a market, we consider prices to be "biased" (as opposed to fair). The PAPM is a model in which markets are beyond efficient and prices are biased.

The idea of including security characteristics and investor attitudes toward them is not new. As we discussed in Chapter 4, Ibbotson, Diermeier, and Siegel (1984) presented a sketch for an equilibrium model based on characteristics and investors' attitudes toward them in their New Equilibrium Theory (NET).

In Chapter 1, we presented a two-part taxonomy of security characteristics that could potentially affect security prices. The two sets of characteristics are *classical* and *behavioral*. Under the classical heading, we further classified characteristics as *risks* or *frictional*. Classical models, such as the CAPM and arbitrage pricing theory, take only the risk characteristics into account. NET extends classical models by taking into account the frictional characteristics, which include taxes, trading costs, and divisibility. The PAPM extends NET by including behavioral characteristics.

The PAPM is relevant in the context of an individual security as well as in an asset allocation context involving allocations to such assets as stocks, corporate and municipal bonds, real estate, and so forth. The characteristics modeled in the PAPM can also represent many of the psychological desires and preferences that are portrayed in behavioral finance—for example, prospect theory, affect, sentiment, and attentiveness. Furthermore, in equity markets, the characteristics function like factor premiums, such as value versus growth, momentum versus reversal, size, quality, liquidity, and even volatility (because, in some instances, investors might even prefer riskier assets).[31] The discovery of these premiums has led to the development of indexes that are investable as "smart" or "strategic" exchange-traded funds. Because in the PAPM such premiums are the result of popularity effects, we identify them with the popularity premiums that we discussed in previous chapters as a way of formally modeling them.

The existence of premiums raises these questions:

- Why do they exist? The existence of premiums, other than the overall equity risk premium, appears to be the "free lunch" that, according to the CAPM, should not exist.

- Which investors are on the opposite side? If some investors are systematically beating the market, then for the market to clear, there must be investors systematically falling behind the market. These investors are the ones Robert Arnott (quoted in Rostad 2013) calls "willing losers" or, by extension, unknowing losers.

To answer these questions, we need a model that

- contains premiums and

- allows for some investors to hold portfolios tilted toward the premiums (who thus outperform the market) and some investors to tilt away from these premiums (who thus underperform the market).

In Chapter 3, we discussed what such a model might look like. In that chapter, we focused on characteristics of securities that we call "dimensions of popularity." The idea is that each security characteristic can be ranked along a popularity continuum. For example, highly liquid stocks are regarded as popular, whereas illiquid stocks are regarded as unpopular. Investors who have a strong demand for popularity hold securities that rank high on the popularity scales and are willing to give up return to do so. Investors who do not demand popularity and who believe that they will be compensated

---

[31]Strictly speaking, factors are systematic drivers of returns that can be captured with long and short combinations of securities with various characteristics, which may or may not be risk related. In the PAPM, the important aspect of the characteristics is not their risk profile but the investor preferences for or against the characteristics, which lead to the premiums in the marketplace.

for holding unpopular stocks hold securities that rank low on the popularity scales and can expect to earn superior returns.

The key to understanding equilibrium pricing in securities is to recognize that securities have both risk and nonrisk characteristics. In the PAPM, investors are risk averse and diversify, as in the CAPM, but they also vary in their preferences toward the other characteristics that securities embody. Securities supply the various characteristics, and investors demand them to varying degrees. As we discussed in Chapter 1, supply does not change as quickly as demand. Thus, the characteristics and, ultimately, the securities are priced according to the weighted average of investor preferences. The investors are proportionally weighted by their wealth but inversely weighted by their risk aversion.

We present the PAPM here by formalizing the ideas that we discussed in Chapter 4 but applying them more broadly. We do this by extending the CAPM to include classical and behavioral security characteristics that different investors regard differently, both positively and negatively. This process leads to an equilibrium in which:

- The expected excess return on each security is a linear function of its beta and its multiple *popularity loadings,* which measure the popularity of the security based on its characteristics relative to those of the beta-adjusted market portfolio.

- Each investor holds a different portfolio based on his or her attitudes toward security characteristics.

- Investor preferences determine the prices of the securities.

The remainder of this chapter is organized as follows. First, we review the CAPM in detail to set the stage for the PAPM. Then, building off the presentation of the CAPM, we present the PAPM in detail. Finally, we present a numerical example to illustrate the differences between the CAPM and the PAPM.

Review of the CAPM

The CAPM makes the following assumptions:

1. Taxes, transaction costs, and other real-world considerations can be ignored.

2. All investors use mean–variance optimization (MVO) as described by Markowitz (1952, 1959, 1987) to select their portfolios.

3. All investors have the same forecasts; that is, they use the same capital market assumptions (expected returns, standard deviations, and correlations) when constructing their portfolios.

4. All investors can borrow and lend at the same risk-free rate without limit.

From these assumptions, the following conclusions emerge:

1. From among all possible portfolios of risky assets, the market portfolio (i.e., the capitalization-weighted combination of all risky assets in the market) maximizes the Sharpe ratio (the expected return in excess of the risk-free rate per unit of total risk). Hence, it is on the efficient frontier.

2. Each investor combines the market portfolio with long or short positions in the risk-free asset (cash). Hence, investors do not actually need to perform MVO to construct optimal portfolios.

3. The expected excess return of each security is proportional to its systematic risk with respect to the market portfolio (beta).

To state Assumption 2 formally, let

n = the number of risky securities in the market
$\vec{\mu}$ = the n-element vector of expected excess returns
Ψ = the $n \times n$ variance–covariance matrix of returns to the risky securities
$\vec{x}_i$ = the n-element vector of investor i's allocations to the risky securities[32]
λ_i = the risk aversion parameter of investor i

Then, investor i's MVO problem is to maximize utility by portfolio selection:

$$\max_{\vec{x}_i} U_i(\vec{x}_i) = \vec{\mu}'\vec{x}_i - \frac{\lambda_i}{2}\vec{x}_i'\Psi\vec{x}_i. \tag{5.1}$$

To state Conclusion 2 formally, let

m = the number of investors
w_i = the fraction of wealth held by investor i; that is, $\sum_{i=1}^{m} w_i = 1$

---

[32]As stated in Assumption 4, there is a risk-free security to which the investor allocates $1 - \sum_{j=1}^{n} x_{ij}$.

Aggregating across investors provides the market level of risk aversion and the market portfolio:[33]

$$\lambda_M = \frac{1}{\sum_{i=1}^{m} \frac{w_i}{\lambda_i}} \tag{5.2}$$

and

$$\vec{\mathbf{x}}_M = \sum_{i=1}^{m} w_i \vec{\mathbf{x}}_i. \tag{5.3}$$

(The M subscript indicates aggregation to the market level.) As we show in Appendix B, each investor holds the market portfolio in proportion to the ratio of his or her risk tolerance (the reciprocal of risk aversion) to the wealth-weighted average risk tolerance:

$$\vec{\mathbf{x}}_i = \frac{\lambda_M}{\lambda_i} \vec{\mathbf{x}}_M. \tag{5.4}$$

In the standard CAPM, the net supply of the risk-free asset (cash) is zero, so $\sum_{j=1}^{n} x_{Mj} = 1$. Thus, Equation 5.4 states that if investor i is less risk averse than the average investor, he or she borrows at the risk-free rate and levers the market portfolio. Conversely, if investor i is more risk averse than the average investor, he or she holds a combination of the risk-free asset (cash) and the market portfolio.

Figure 5.1 illustrates Conclusions 1 and 2 graphically. It shows that in the CAPM, the market portfolio is on the MVO efficient frontier. Its location is the point of tangency between the capital market line and the efficient frontier. The capital market line is the line of tangency that emanates from the risk-free rate on the vertical axis. As Figure 5.1 shows, not only is the market portfolio on the capital market line but so are the portfolios of all investors. Investors who take more risk than the market portfolio have portfolios above it, indicating that they hold levered positions in it. Investors who take less risk than the market portfolio have portfolios below it, indicating that they hold delevered positions in it.

---

[33]Note that the market aggregation of risk aversion is the weighted harmonic mean (reciprocal of the arithmetic mean of the reciprocals) of the risk aversion of the investors.

Figure 5.1. Equilibrium in the CAPM

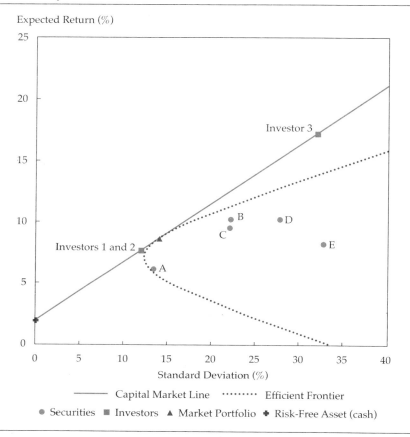

To state Conclusion 3 formally, define the expected excess return on the market portfolio as

$$\mu_M = \vec{x}'_M \vec{\mu}. \tag{5.5}$$

Define the variance of the market portfolio as

$$\sigma^2_M = \vec{x}'_M \Psi \vec{x}_M. \tag{5.6}$$

The familiar CAPM equation for expected excess returns can be written as

$$\vec{\mu} = \vec{\beta}\mu_M, \tag{5.7}$$

where

$$\vec{\beta} = \frac{\Psi \vec{x}_M}{\sigma_M^2}. \tag{5.8}$$

In other words, the expected excess return on each security is the product of its systematic risk with respect to the market portfolio (beta) and the expected excess return of the market portfolio.

Single-Period Valuation in the CAPM. So far, we have given the conventional presentation of the CAPM as a model of portfolio construction and expected return. The CAPM is also, however, a *single-period* valuation model (which is why it is called an "asset pricing" model). Let

v_j = the current market value of security j
$\tilde{y}_j$ = the exogenous random end-of-period total value of security j
r_f = the risk-free rate

The current value of each security j can then be written as

$$v_j = \frac{E[\tilde{y}_j]}{1 + r_f + \beta_j \mu_M}. \tag{5.9}$$

The expected end-of-period value of each security, $E[\tilde{y}_j]$, is, in a sense, the *fundamental* of the security that the market prices.[34] If all securities had the same systematic risk (beta), the denominator of Equation 5.9 would be the same for all securities and all market values would be proportional to this fundamental. But not all securities have the same systematic risk, so the market value of a security depends both on its fundamental and on its risk.

Equation 5.9 corresponds to the most common way that valuation is carried out—namely, by discounting the expected value of future cash flows (the numerator) by a risk-adjusted discount rate (the denominator). Another way to approach valuation, however, is to risk-adjust expected future flows (the fundamental) and then discount the risk-adjusted value by the risk-free rate. To demonstrate, let

$\tilde{y}_M$ = the random end-of-period value of the market as a whole
v_M = the value of the market as whole

---

[34]We are using the term "fundamental" in the sense used by Arnott, Hsu, and Moore (2005): a characteristic of a company that is indicative of the company's economic footprint that is independent of market value.

61

By definition,

$$v_M = \sum_{j=1}^{n} v_i.$$ (5.10)

Let $\tilde{\mathbf{y}}$ denote the vector of random exogenous end-of-period total security values. Then, the distribution of $\tilde{\mathbf{y}}$ constitutes the real economy. Denote the variance–covariance matrix of $\tilde{\mathbf{y}}$ as Ω. The systematic risk of an individual end-of-period security value $\tilde{y}_j$ with respect to total economic output ($\sum_{i=1}^{n} \tilde{y}_i$) is the covariance of the economic output of j with that of all other economic output divided by the variance of total economic output:

$$\gamma_j = \frac{\sum_{i=1}^{n} \Omega_{ij}}{\sum_{i=1}^{n} \sum_{k=1}^{n} \Omega_{ik}}.$$ (5.11)

The systematic risk of the value of economic output, γ_j, is related to the systematic risk of return, β_j, as follows:

$$\gamma_j = x_{Mj}\beta_j.$$ (5.12)

As we show in Appendix B, the value of security j can be expressed as:

$$v_j = \frac{E[\tilde{y}_j] - v_M \gamma_j \mu_M}{1 + r_f}.$$ (5.13)

Although Equation 5.13 yields the same results as Equation 5.9, as we will show, the valuation equation that we derive for the PAPM is a generalization of Equation 5.9.

The Popularity Asset Pricing Model

The PAPM is a generalization of the CAPM in which securities have characteristics other than risk and expected return that investors are concerned about. Its assumptions are as follows:

1. Each security has a bundle of characteristics.

2. Investors have preferences regarding these characteristics in addition to their preferences regarding risk and expected return.

3. All investors use a generalized form of MVO that incorporates their preferences regarding security characteristics.

4. All investors have the same forecasts; that is, they hold the same capital market assumptions (expected returns, standard deviations, and correlations).

5. All investors agree on what the characteristics of the securities are.

6. All investors can borrow and lend at the same risk-free rate without limit.

The conclusions of the PAPM are as follows:

1. The market portfolio does *not* maximize the Sharpe ratio among all portfolios of risk assets.

2. Each investor forms a customized portfolio of the risky assets that reflects his or her attitudes toward each security characteristic. This portfolio is combined with long or short positions in the risk-free asset. Portfolio optimization is required to find the overall investor-specific portfolio.

3. The expected excess return of each security is a linear function of its beta and its popularity loadings, which measure the popularity of the security based on its characteristics relative to those of the beta-adjusted market portfolio. The popularity loadings are multiplied by the popularity premiums, which are aggregations of the preferences of the investors regarding the characteristics. In this way, the market aggregates investor preferences in determining the influence of security characteristics on the expected returns and prices of the securities.

Note that the conclusions of the PAPM are nearly the exact opposite of those of the CAPM. Additionally, Conclusion 2 is much more consistent with observed investor portfolios.

Figure 5.2 illustrates Conclusions 1 and 2. The market portfolio is not on the Sharpe ratio–maximizing tangent line. Neither are the portfolios of Investors 1 and 2, as is the case in the CAPM. Investor 3's portfolio, however, is on the tangent line. This investor is risk averse but has no other preferences for security characteristics and, therefore, holds an efficient portfolio. We present the specifics of this example in the next section.

To state Assumptions 2–4 formally, let

p = the number of characteristics (besides risk and expected excess return)
$\mathbf{C}$ = $n \times p$ matrix of characteristics of the securities (or asset classes)
$\bar{\varphi}_i$ = p-element vector of investor i's attitudes toward the characteristics

(The elements can be positive or negative.)

Figure 5.2. Equilibrium under the PAPM

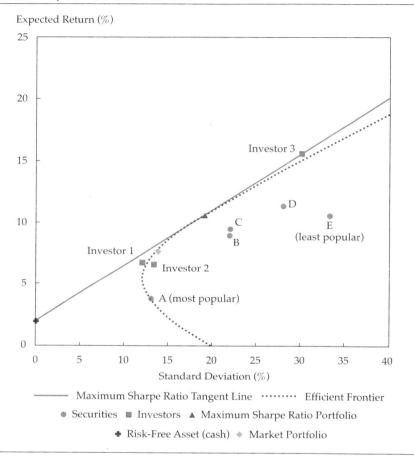

Investor i's problem is the following:

$$\max_{\vec{x}_i} U_i(\vec{x}_i) = \vec{\mu}'\vec{x}_i + \vec{\varphi}_i'C'\vec{x}_i - \frac{\lambda_i}{2}\vec{x}_i'\Psi\vec{x}_i, \qquad (5.14)$$

which is the utility-maximization problem introduced in Chapter 4 to formalize the main idea of NET. Here, however, the nonrisk characteristics are not only the costs that rational investors care about, such as liquidity, but also characteristics that investors desire for irrational reasons, such as the popularity of the companies that issue the stock. In the NET framework, where all of the nonrisk characteristics are costs, the elements of $\vec{\varphi}_i$ are all negative.

But, in the more general PAPM, the elements of $\vec{\varphi}_i$ that are on characteristics that the investor likes are positive.

This extension of MVO is similar to the formulation in Cooper, Evnine, Finkelman, Huntington, and Lynch (2016). The main difference is in interpretation. In Cooper et al., the nonrisk characteristics are expected social-impact metrics (ESG factors), whereas in the PAPM, the nonrisk characteristics can include these factors but can also include any number of other security characteristics that investors might care about.

Note that because the preferences for characteristics enter the utility function in parallel with expected returns, they should be in the same units. For example, if $\varphi_{11} = 5\%$, Investor 1 would be indifferent between a 100% allocation to a security with exposure of 1.0 to characteristic 1 and a 5% increase in expected return.

The solution to the maximization problem shown in Equation 5.14 is

$$\vec{x}_i = \frac{1}{\lambda_i} \Psi^{-1}(\vec{\mu} + \mathbf{C}\vec{\varphi}_i). \tag{5.15}$$

As we show in Appendix C, each investor's portfolio can be expressed in terms of the market portfolio and the investor's attitudes toward security characteristics:

$$\vec{x}_i = \frac{\lambda_M}{\lambda_i} \vec{x}_M + \frac{1}{\lambda_i} \Psi^{-1}\mathbf{C}(\vec{\varphi}_i - \vec{\pi}), \tag{5.16}$$

where $\vec{\pi}$ denotes the vector of the aggregation of investor attitudes toward the characteristics:

$$\vec{\pi} = \lambda_M \sum_{i=1}^{m} \frac{w_i}{\lambda_i} \vec{\varphi}_i. \tag{5.17}$$

For reasons that will become apparent, we call $\vec{\pi}$ the vector of *popularity premiums*.

Equation 5.16 shows how each investor's portfolio differs from the market portfolio based on (1) the investor's attitude toward risk and (2) his or her attitude toward security characteristics.

In Appendix C, we show that expected excess returns can be written as

$$\vec{\mu} = \vec{\beta}\mu_M + (\vec{\beta}\vec{c}'_M - \mathbf{C})\vec{\pi}, \tag{5.18}$$

where $\vec{\mathbf{c}}_M = \mathbf{C}'\vec{\mathbf{x}}_M$.

Equation 5.18 looks like a multifactor asset pricing model but with popularity premiums rather than risk premiums. Let

$$\delta_{jk} = \beta_j c_{Mj} - C_{jk} \tag{5.19}$$

so we can write

$$\mu_j = \beta_j \mu_M + \sum_{k=1}^{p} \delta_{jk} \pi_k. \tag{5.20}$$

Separating out the risk-free rate, we can write Equation 5.20 as an equation for the expected total return of security *j*:

$$E[\tilde{r}_j] = r_f + \beta_j \mu_M + \sum_{k=1}^{p} \delta_{jk} \pi_k. \tag{5.21}$$

Equation 5.21 is of the same form as the Popularity formula for expected return in Figure 3.3 that we postulated would hold in an equilibrium in which investors care about nonrisk characteristics. The main difference is that in the formula in Figure 3.3, we have proxies for such characteristics as market cap (size) and market-based measures of value, whereas in Equation 5.21 we have the actual characteristics.

We call δ_{jk} security *j*'s "popularity loading" on characteristic *k*. It is positive if security *j*'s exposure to characteristic *k* is less than that of the beta-adjusted market portfolio and negative if the reverse is true. In this way, a popularity loading of a security is positive for a given characteristic if the security is unpopular with respect to the characteristic and negative if it is popular.

As a special case, the net attitude toward characteristics could be zero ($\bar{\pi} = 0$), so the CAPM equation for expected excess returns would still prevail and the market portfolio would be mean–variance efficient. Even in that case, however, each investor still tilts his or her portfolio toward the preferred characteristics and away from the ones disliked, as described by Equation 5.16.

Valuation under the PAPM. Just as the equation for expected excess returns in the CAPM can be used to derive a one-period valuation formula (Equation 5.13), so Equation 5.18 can be used to derive a valuation formula for the PAPM.

In Appendix C, we derive the following PAPM valuation formula:

$$v_j = \frac{E[\tilde{y}_j] - \gamma_j v_M (\mu_M + \vec{c}_M' \vec{\pi})}{1 + r_f - \vec{c}_j' \vec{\pi}}. \tag{5.22}$$

Equation 5.22 shows the respective roles that systematic risk (as measured by γ_j) and nonrisk characteristics ($\vec{c}_j$) play in determining the market value of a security when the PAPM is used. As can be seen from the numerator in Equation 5.22, systematic risk reduces the value of the security, much in the same way that it does in the CAPM (see Equation B.22 in Appendix B). Systematic risk is part of a term deducted from the security's fundamental, $E[\tilde{y}_j]$. In contrast, the nonrisk characteristics appear in the denominator where, multiplied by the popularity premiums, they form deductions from the risk-free rate. In this way, the market value of a security depends on both its risk and nonrisk characteristics.

A Numerical Example

To create Figure 5.1 and Figure 5.2, we used an example with five securities and three investors. **Table 5.1** presents the assumptions regarding the joint distribution of the end-of-period values of five securities. This is the model of the real economy in our example. To keep the example simple, we assume that there is one characteristic that investors care about, called popularity, which we also show in Table 5.1.

Table 5.2 presents the assumptions regarding the investors. Note that Investor 3 has a popularity preference of zero; she is indifferent to whether a security is popular or not. This investor's portfolio is on the tangent line in Figure 5.2.

Table 5.1. Assumptions about Popularity and the Real Economy for Five Hypothetical Securities

Security	Popularity	Expected Value ($)	Standard Deviation ($)	A	B	C	D	E
				Correlation of End-of-Period Value with:				
A	0.50	10	1.3	1.0				
B	0.25	8	1.6	0.4	1.0			
C	0.00	6	1.2	0.3	0.4	1.0		
D	−0.25	4	1.0	0.2	0.3	0.4	1.0	
E	−0.50	1	0.3	0.1	0.2	0.3	0.4	1.0

Table 5.2. Assumptions Regarding Investors

Description	Investor 1	Investor 2	Investor 3	Market
Fraction of market $ wealth (w_j)	60%	30%	10%	100%
Risk aversion (λ_j)	4.00	4.00	1.50	3.43
Popularity preference (ϕ_j)[a]	5.0%	7.5%	0.0%	4.5%

[a]We scaled the popularity preferences in this example to be in the same units as expected returns.

In addition to the assumptions presented in Tables 5.1 and 5.2, we assume that the risk-free rate is 2%.

We solved the model under the assumptions of the CAPM (all popularity preferences set to zero) and under the assumptions of the PAPM by using the techniques described in Appendixes B and C, respectively. **Table 5.3** and **Table 5.4** present the results.

In Chapter 3, we introduced the concept of a market that is "beyond efficient" in which prices are "biased," as opposed to "fair" in an "efficient market." With this numerical example of the CAPM (an efficient market model) and the PAPM (a model in which the market is beyond efficient), we can measure the pricing biases. In the last column of Table 5.3, we show the percentage difference between the PAPM and CAPM value of each security and of the market as a whole. These percentages are the pricing biases. As expected, the prices of the popular securities are biased up and the prices of the unpopular securities are biased down relative to their fair values under the CAPM.

In **Figure 5.3**, we show the popularity characteristic versus the pricing biases shown in the last column of Table 5.3. Figure 5.3 reveals that not only

Table 5.3. Expected Returns and Valuations under the CAPM and the PAPM

Security	Expected Return		Value ($)		Pricing Bias
	CAPM	PAPM	CAPM	PAPM	
A	6.23%	3.85%	9.41	9.63	2.29%
B	10.33	9.03	7.25	7.34	1.19
C	9.62	9.54	5.47	5.48	0.07
D	10.25	11.38	3.63	3.59	−1.02
E	8.28	10.61	0.92	0.90	−2.10
Market	8.66	7.65	26.69	26.94	0.94

Table 5.4.   Investor and Market Portfolios under the CAPM and the PAPM

Security/ Statistic	Investor 1		Investor 2		Investor 3		Market	
	CAPM	PAPM	CAPM	PAPM	CAPM	PAPM	CAPM	PAPM
A	30%	35%	30%	55%	81%	−17%	35%	36%
B	23	23	23	24	62	59	27	27
C	18	17	18	16	47	54	21	20
D	12	11	12	9	31	42	14	13
E	3	2	3	0	8	20	3	3
Cash	14	11	14	−3	−139	−58	0	0
Expected return	7.71	6.82	7.71	6.68	17.22	15.56	8.66	7.65
Standard deviation	11.94	12.02	11.94	13.28	31.85	30.06	13.93	13.81

Figure 5.3.   The Popularity Characteristic vs. Pricing Bias

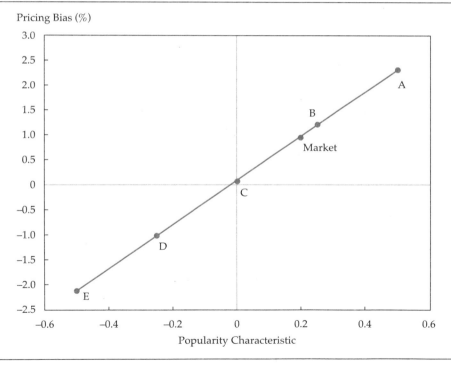

is there a positive relationship between popularity and pricing bias but also the relationship is nearly linear.

These results reveal two striking features. First, from Table 5.3, we see that. although values of the securities are similar in both models, the expected returns are quite different. The reason is that expected returns are highly sensitive to changes in value because of their inversely proportional relationship:

$$\mu_j + r_f = \frac{E[\tilde{y}_j]}{v_j} - 1. \tag{5.23}$$

Because $v_j < E[\tilde{y}_j]$, the sensitivity is high. **Figure 5.4** illustrates this sensitivity by showing how the expected return of Security E changes as the value of the security changes. (The curve appears to be linear rather than hyperbolic because the figure plots only a tiny part of the curve.)

The second striking feature is the radical change that Investor 3 undergoes in moving from the CAPM world to the PAPM world. As you can see

Figure 5.4. Relationship between the Value and Expected Return of Unpopular Security E

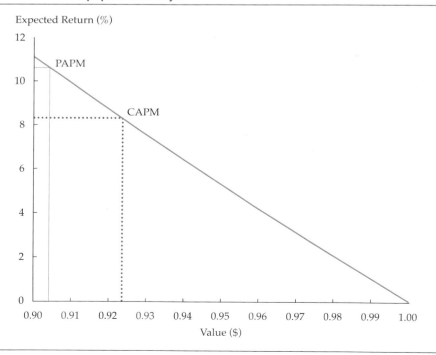

Table 5.5. The Portfolio with the Maximum Sharpe Ratio under the CAPM and the PAPM

Security/Statistic	CAPM	PAPM
A	35%	−11%
B	27%	37%
C	21%	34%
D	14%	26%
E	3%	13%
Expected return	8.66%	10.58%
Standard deviation	13.93%	19.03%
Sharpe ratio	0.48	0.45

from Table 5.2, Investor 3 pays no attention to the nonrisk characteristic and, therefore, focuses entirely on risk and expected return. For this reason, Investor 3's portfolio is on the tangent line in Figure 5.2. Because Investor 3 is much less risk averse than Investors 1 and 2, in the scenarios of both the CAPM and the PAPM, she takes on a lot of leverage. But the levered portfolios are quite different. In the CAPM, she levers the market portfolio. But in the PAPM, she holds a levered position in the Sharpe-ratio-maximizing portfolio, shown in **Table 5.5**, which is *short* in the most popular security, Security A. As Table 5.4 shows, Security A is attractive to Investors 1 and 2 because of their preferences for popular stocks, but Investor 3, who has no preference regarding popularity, takes advantage of their preferences by shorting it. Thus, she follows a "risk arbitrage strategy" by going short the most popular security and going long the less popular ones.[35]

This example illustrates how in the PAPM, where investors hold custom portfolios based on how much they care about (or do not care about) popularity characteristics, investors can be thought of as forming clienteles for the dimensions of popularity. For example, Investor 2, who has the strongest preference for the popularity characteristic, has 55% of his portfolio in the most popular security (Security A); Investor 3, who has no preference for the popularity characteristic, holds substantially more of the least popular security (Security E) than the other investors and the market as a whole.

---

[35]Unlike a true arbitrage strategy, a risk arbitrage strategy is, of course, risky. Over the long run, however, so long as the risk arbitrager can identify which securities are likely to outperform (in this example, because they are unpopular) and which are likely to underperform, the strategy should yield a profit. Damodaran (undated) calls such a strategy "speculative arbitrage," perhaps a more revealing name than "risk arbitrage."

Table 5.6. Expected Return Equations under the CAPM and the PAPM

	CAPM $E[\tilde{r}_j] = r_f + \beta_j \mu_M$ $= 2.00\% + \beta_j 6.66\%$			PAPM $E[\tilde{r}_j] = r_f + \beta_j \mu_M + \delta_j \pi$ $= 2.00\% + \beta_j 5.65\% + \delta_j 4.50\%$		
Security	Beta	Expected Return	Beta	Popularity Loading	Expected Return
A	0.64	6.23%	0.63	−0.38	3.85%
B	1.25	10.33	1.25	0.00	9.03
C	1.14	9.62	1.15	0.23	9.54
D	1.24	10.25	1.26	0.50	11.38
E	0.94	8.28	0.97	0.69	10.61
Market	1.00	8.66	1.00	0.00	7.65

Finally, **Table 5.6** compares the equations for expected returns under the CAPM and under the PAPM. Note that the most popular security (A), has a negative popularity loading. Also note that the three least popular securities (C, D, and E) have positive popularity loadings, so these securities can be categorized as popular. In addition, note that under the PAPM, differences in popularity loadings lead to differences in expected returns larger than would be expected based only on the differences in betas. For example, Security E has a higher expected return than Security B (10.61% vs. 9.03%), even though Security E has a much lower beta than Security B (0.97 vs. 1.25).[36] This result is consistent with many empirical findings that differences in betas do not explain differences in returns, and it demonstrates how the theory of popularity can explain this phenomenon.

Conclusion

Equilibrium asset pricing models, such as the CAPM, predict that expected returns on securities will be linear functions of systematic risk factors. A large body of empirical evidence suggests, however, that premiums are related to characteristics not related to risk. Hence, we need a new model that takes nonrisk characteristics into account. In this chapter, we presented such a model, the popularity asset pricing model. ·

---

[36]Even though Security E is the least popular and has the highest standard deviation of return, it does not have the highest expected return. Rather, Security D, which is the second least popular, has the highest expected return. This is because its much higher beta (1.26 vs. 0.97) more than makes up for the difference in popularity.

We formed the PAPM by extending the CAPM to include preferences for nonrisk security characteristics in investor objective functions. In the PAPM, an equilibrium emerges in which the expected excess return of each security is a linear function of its systematic risk with respect to the market portfolio (beta) and its popularity loadings, which measure the popularity of the security based on its characteristics relative to those of the beta-adjusted market portfolio. As we illustrated, differences in popularity loadings can cause differences in expected returns greater than would be expected if we consider only differences in betas. The coefficients on the popularity loadings—the popularity premiums—are the aggregated attitudes of investors toward the nonrisk security characteristics. Furthermore, the market portfolio does not maximize the Sharpe ratio; it is merely the aggregation across investors of each investor's customized portfolio.

We illustrated that an investor who has only risk aversion preferences can benefit by loading up on the less popular securities. This investor can also use leverage and potentially short the most popular securities. But no risk-free arbitrage exists in the PAPM framework. The investor, or clientele of similar investors, can influence market prices but not remove the effect of popularity. The market is made up of all its participants, with each of them affecting prices and expected returns.

These conclusions have important practical implications. First, when estimating the equity cost of capital, adjustments need to be made for the characteristics of the security in question. Second, the conclusions imply that by focusing only on expected return and risk, an investor may be able to create portfolios that are more efficient than market-weighted indexes. Thus, one can profit by trading against investors who take into account security characteristics other than risk.

The approach that we took in constructing the PAPM can be extended to take into account other types of heterogeneity among investors. For example, investors could have heterogeneous views about the expected value of the real economic output associated with each security, much as in Lintner (1969). In general, deriving the equilibrium of a model with investors who are heterogeneous in different respects should be possible.

Appendix B. Formal Presentation of the CAPM

Investor i's problem is as follows:

$$\max_{\vec{\mathbf{x}}_i} U_i(\vec{\mathbf{x}}_i) = \vec{\mu}'\vec{\mathbf{x}}_i - \frac{\lambda_i}{2}\vec{\mathbf{x}}_i'\Psi\vec{\mathbf{x}}_i. \tag{B.1}$$

where

$\bar{\mu}$ = the n-element vector of expected excess returns
Ψ = the $n \times n$ variance–covariance matrix of returns to the risky securities
$\bar{x}_i$ = the n-element vector of investor i's allocations to the risky securities
λ_i = the risk aversion parameter of investor i

From the first-order condition, we have

$$\bar{\mu} = \lambda_i \Psi \bar{x}_i. \tag{B.2}$$

Solving for $\bar{x}_i$, we have

$$\bar{x}_i = \frac{1}{\lambda_i} \Psi^{-1} \bar{\mu}. \tag{B.3}$$

Let m be the number of investors and w_i be the fraction of wealth held by investor i; $\sum_{i=1}^{m} w_i = 1$. Aggregating across investors, we have the market level of risk aversion and the market portfolio:

$$\lambda_M = \frac{1}{\sum_{i=1}^{m} \frac{w_i}{\lambda_i}} \tag{B.4}$$

and

$$\bar{x}_M = \sum_{i=1}^{m} w_i \bar{x}_i, \tag{B.5}$$

where the M subscript indicates the market.

Aggregating Equation B.3 across investors, we have

$$\bar{x}_M = \frac{1}{\lambda_M} \Psi^{-1} \bar{\mu}. \tag{B.6}$$

So,

$$\bar{\mu} = \lambda_M \Psi \bar{x}_M. \tag{B.7}$$

From Equations B.3 and B.6, we can see that each investor holds the market portfolio in proportion to the ratio of the wealth-weighted average risk aversion to his or her risk aversion:

$$\vec{\mathbf{x}}_i = \frac{\lambda_M}{\lambda_i} \vec{\mathbf{x}}_M. \tag{B.8}$$

In the standard CAPM, the net supply of the risk-free asset is zero, so $\sum_{j=1}^{n} x_{Mj} = 1$. Therefore, Equation B.8 tells us that if investor i is less risk averse that the average investor, he or she borrows at the risk-free rate and levers the market portfolio. Conversely, if investor i is more risk averse than the average investor, she or he holds a combination of the risk-free asset (cash) and the market portfolio.

Expected Excess Returns under the CAPM. The expected excess return on the market portfolio is

$$\mu_M = \vec{\mathbf{x}}'_M \vec{\mu}. \tag{B.9}$$

Hence, multiplying Equation B.7 through by $\vec{\mathbf{x}}_M$ yields

$$\mu_M = \lambda_M \sigma_M^2, \tag{B.10}$$

where $\sigma_M^2 = \vec{\mathbf{x}}'_M \mathbf{\Psi} \vec{\mathbf{x}}_M$. This is the variance of the market portfolio.
From Equation B.10, it follows that

$$\lambda_M = \frac{\mu_M}{\sigma_M^2}. \tag{B.11}$$

Substituting the right-hand side of Equation B.11 for λ_M in Equation B.7 and rearranging terms yields the familiar CAPM equation for expected excess returns:

$$\vec{\mu} = \vec{\beta} \mu_M, \tag{B.12}$$

where

$$\vec{\beta} = \frac{\mathbf{\Psi} \vec{\mathbf{x}}_M}{\sigma_M^2}. \tag{B.13}$$

Valuation under the CAPM. Because the CAPM is a one-period model, the value of each security j can be written as

$$v_j = \frac{E[\tilde{y}_j]}{1 + r_f + \beta_j \mu_M},$$ (B.14)

where

v_j = the total market value of security j
$\tilde{y}_j$ = the random exogenous end-of-period total value of security j
r_f = the risk-free rate

Let $\tilde{y}_M$ be the random end-of-period value of the market as a whole and v_M be the value of the market as whole. Then, by definition

$$\tilde{y}_M = \sum_{j=1}^{n} \tilde{y}_j,$$ (B.15)

$$v_M = \sum_{j=1}^{n} v_i,$$ (B.16)

and

$$x_{Mj} = \frac{v_j}{v_M}.$$ (B.17)

The realized total return on security j is

$$\tilde{r}_j = \frac{\tilde{y}_j}{v_j} - 1.$$ (B.18)

Let $\tilde{\tilde{y}}$ denote the vector of random end-of-period total security values. The distribution of $\tilde{\tilde{y}}$ constitutes the real economy. Denote the variance–covariance matrix of $\tilde{\tilde{y}}$ as Ω. From the definition of Ω and Equation B.15, it follows that the jq element of the variance–covariance matrix of returns, Ψ, can be written as:

$$\Psi_{jq} = \frac{\Omega_{jq}}{v_j v_q}.$$ (B.19)

So, the formula for β_j can be rewritten as follows:

$$\begin{aligned}
\beta_j &= \frac{\sum_{i=1}^{n} \Psi_{ij} x_i}{\sum_{i=1}^{n} \sum_{k=1}^{n} \Psi_{ik} x_i x_k} \\
&= \frac{1/v_j}{1/v_M} \frac{\sum_{i=1}^{n} \Omega_{ij}}{\sum_{i=1}^{n} \sum_{k=1}^{n} \Omega_{ik}} \\
&= \frac{\gamma_j}{x_{Mj}},
\end{aligned} \tag{B.20}$$

where

$$\gamma_j = \frac{\sum_{q=1}^{n} \Omega_{jq}}{\sum_{q=1}^{n} \sum_{s=1}^{n} \Omega_{qs}}. \tag{B.21}$$

Substituting the final term in Equation B.20 for β_j in Equation B.14, rearranging terms, and simplifying yields the following equation for the total value of security j

$$v_j = \frac{E[\tilde{y}_j] - v_M \gamma_j \mu_M}{1 + r_f}. \tag{B.22}$$

The value of the market as a whole is

$$v_M = \frac{E[\tilde{y}_M]}{1 + \mu_M + r_f}. \tag{B.23}$$

Substituting the right-hand side of Equation B.23 for v_M in Equation B.22 yields:

$$v_j = \frac{E[\tilde{y}_j] - E[\tilde{y}_M]\gamma_j \dfrac{\mu_M}{1 + \mu_M + r_f}}{1 + r_f}. \tag{B.24}$$

Solving the CAPM. Equation B.24 states the values of the risky securities in terms of the underlying economic variables ($\tilde{\mathbf{y}}$), the market risk premium (μ_M), and the risk-free rate (r_f). From these values, we can derive all of the other variables in the CAPM by using the earlier equations. We take the risk-free rate as given; we still need to solve for the market risk premium.

The market risk premium depends on the market risk aversion. To see exactly how, first consider what Equation B.21 implies about the variance of return on the market portfolio, σ_M^2:

$$
\sigma_M^2 = \sum_{i=1}^{n} \sum_{j=1}^{n} x_{Mi} x_{Mj} \Psi_{ij}
$$

$$
= \sum_{i=1}^{n} \sum_{j=1}^{n} \frac{\Omega_{ij}}{v_M^2} \tag{B.25}
$$

$$
= \frac{\mathrm{Var}[\tilde{y}_M]}{v_M^2}.
$$

Substituting the right-hand side of Equation B.23 for v_M in Equation B.25 yields

$$
\sigma_M^2 = \frac{(1 + r_f + \mu_M)^2}{\kappa}, \tag{B.26}
$$

where

$$
\kappa = \frac{E[\tilde{y}_M]^2}{\mathrm{Var}[\tilde{y}_M]}. \tag{B.27}
$$

Substituting the right-hand side of Equation B.10 for σ_M^2 in Equation B.26 and rearranging terms yields a quadratic equation for μ_M:

$$
\mu_M^2 + \left[2(1 + r_f) - \frac{\kappa}{\lambda_M} \right] \mu_M + (1 + r_f)^2 = 0. \tag{B.28}
$$

The relevant solution is as follows:

$$
\mu_M = \frac{\kappa \lambda_M - 2(1 + r_f) - \sqrt{\left[2(1 + r_f) - \dfrac{\kappa}{\lambda_M} \right]^2 - 4(1 + r_f)^2}}{2}. \tag{B.29}
$$

Figure B.1.   Relationship between Market Risk Aversion and the Market Risk Premium under the CAPM

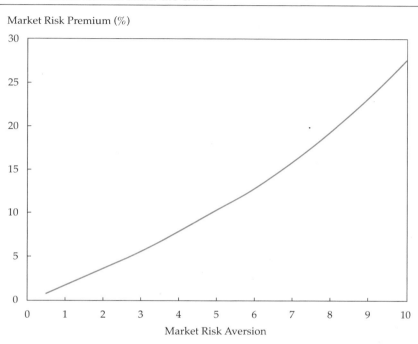

Equation B.29 is, in effect, the solution to the CAPM.

Figure B.1 is a plot showing the relationship between market risk aversion (λ_M) and the market risk premium (μ_M), taking the risk-free rate (r_p) and the parameters of the distribution of total market end-of-period value (κ) as given. The relationship is positive, so the higher the higher the level of market risk aversion, the higher the market risk premium.

Appendix C. Formal Presentation of the PAPM

Let

   p = the number of popularity characteristics
   $\mathbf{C}$ = $n \times p$ matrix of characteristics of the securities
   $\bar{\varphi}_i$ = p-element vector of investor i's attitudes toward the characteristics
       (The elements can be positive or negative.)

Investor i's problem is as follows:

$$\max_{\vec{\mathbf{x}}_i} U_i(\vec{\mathbf{x}}_i) = \vec{\mu}'\vec{\mathbf{x}}_i + \vec{\varphi}_i'\mathbf{C}'\vec{\mathbf{x}}_i - \frac{\lambda_i}{2}\vec{\mathbf{x}}_i'\Psi\vec{\mathbf{x}}_i. \tag{C.1}$$

From the first-order condition, we have

$$\vec{\mu} = \lambda_i\Psi\vec{\mathbf{x}}_i - \mathbf{C}\vec{\varphi}_i. \tag{C.2}$$

The solution is

$$\vec{\mathbf{x}}_i = \frac{1}{\lambda_i}\Psi^{-1}(\vec{\mu} + \mathbf{C}\vec{\varphi}_i). \tag{C.3}$$

Aggregating Equation C.3 across investors, we have

$$\vec{\mathbf{x}}_M = \frac{1}{\lambda_M}\Psi^{-1}(\vec{\mu} + \mathbf{C}\vec{\pi}), \tag{C.4}$$

where

$$\vec{\pi} = \lambda_M\sum_{i=1}^{m}\frac{w_i}{\lambda_i}\vec{\varphi}_i. \tag{C.5}$$

For reasons that will become apparent, we call $\vec{\pi}$ the vector of *popularity premiums*.

From Equations C.3 and C.4, we derive an equation for the portfolio decision of each investor relative to the market portfolio:

$$\vec{\mathbf{x}}_i = \frac{\lambda_M}{\lambda_i}\vec{\mathbf{x}}_M + \frac{1}{\lambda_i}\Psi^{-1}\mathbf{C}(\vec{\varphi}_i - \vec{\pi}). \tag{C.6}$$

Solving Equation C.4 for $\vec{\mu}$ yields

$$\vec{\mu} = \lambda_M\Psi\vec{\mathbf{x}}_M - \mathbf{C}\vec{\pi}. \tag{C.7}$$

Multiplying Equation C.7 through by $\vec{\mathbf{x}}_M'$ yields

$$\mu_M = \lambda_M\sigma_M^2 - \vec{\mathbf{c}}_M'\vec{\pi}, \tag{C.8}$$

where $\vec{c}_M = \mathbf{C}'\vec{x}_M$. This is the vector of characteristics of the market portfolio. From Equation C.8, it follows that

$$\lambda_M = \frac{\mu_M + \vec{c}'_M \vec{\pi}}{\sigma^2_M}. \tag{C.9}$$

Substituting the right-hand side of Equation C.9 for λ_M in Equation C.7 and rearranging terms yields the generalization of the CAPM equation for expected excess returns:

$$\vec{\mu} = \vec{\beta}\mu_M + (\vec{\beta}\vec{c}'_M - \mathbf{C})\vec{\pi}. \tag{C.10}$$

Equation C.10 looks like a multifactor asset pricing model but with the popularity premiums rather than risk premiums. Let

$$\delta_{jk} = \beta_j c_{Mj} - C_{jk}, \tag{C.11}$$

so we can write

$$\mu_j = \beta_j \mu_M + \sum_{k=1}^{p} \delta_{jk} \pi_j. \tag{C.12}$$

We call δ_{jk} security j's "popularity loading" on characteristic k. It is positive if security j's exposure to characteristic k is less than that of the beta-adjusted market portfolio and negative if the reverse is true. In this way, a popularity loading of a security is positive for a given characteristic if the security is unpopular with respect to the characteristic and negative if it is popular.

As a special case, the net attitude toward popularity characteristics could be zero ($\vec{\pi} = 0$), so the CAPM equation for expected excess returns would still prevail and the market portfolio would be mean–variance efficient. But even in that case, each investor still tilts his or her portfolio toward the preferred characteristics and away from the disliked ones, as described by Equation C.6.

Valuation in the PAPM. Just as the equation for expected excess returns in the CAPM can be used to derive a one-period valuation formula (Equation B.20), Equation C.10 can be used to derive a valuation formula in the PAPM.

To accomplish this derivation, first we write Equation C.10 for a single security as follows:

$$\mu_j = \beta_j(\mu_M + \vec{c}'_M \vec{\pi}) - \vec{c}'_j \vec{\pi}, \tag{C.13}$$

where $\vec{c}_j$ is the vector formed from the jth row of $\mathbf{C}$.

Equations B.17 and B.20 hold under the PAPM just as they do for the CAPM. From them, we have

$$\beta_j = \frac{\gamma_j}{x_j}$$

$$= \frac{\gamma_j v_M}{v_j}, \tag{C.14}$$

where γ_j is as defined in Equation B.21.

The value of security j can be written as

$$v_j = \frac{E[\tilde{y}_j]}{1 + r_f + \mu_j}. \tag{C.15}$$

Substituting the right-hand side of Equation C.13 for μ_j in Equation C.15, rearranging terms, and solving for v_j yields the valuation equation presented as Equation 5.22 in the main text:

$$v_j = \frac{E[\tilde{y}_j] - \gamma_j v_M(\mu_M + \vec{c}'_M \vec{\pi})}{1 + r_f - \vec{c}'_j \vec{\pi}}. \tag{C.16}$$

Solving the PAPM. Unlike the CAPM, the PAPM has no closed-form solution. Instead, to solve it, we need to solve a system of nonlinear equations.

Let $\vec{f}(.)$ denote the n-element vector-valued function that we are seeking to set to $\vec{0}$ by finding the value of the vector of security values, $\vec{v}$, that does so. That is, we seek the solution to

$$\vec{f}(\vec{v}) = \vec{0}. \tag{C.17}$$

Once the solution is found, all of the values of the variables of the model can be derived from the values of $\vec{v}$ and the preceding equations in this appendix.

The values of $\vec{\mathbf{f}}(\vec{\mathbf{v}})$ are determined by making the following set of calculations:

$$\vec{\mathbf{x}}_{M1} = \frac{\vec{\mathbf{v}}}{\sum_{j=1}^{n} v_j}, \tag{C.18}$$

$$\mathbf{\Psi}^{-1} = \mathrm{diag}(\vec{\mathbf{v}})\mathbf{\Omega}^{-1}\mathrm{diag}(\vec{\mathbf{v}}), \tag{C.19}$$

$$\mu_j = \frac{E[\tilde{y}_j]}{v_j} - (1 + r_f), \ \text{for} \ j = 1, 2, \ldots, n, \tag{C.20}$$

$$\vec{\mathbf{x}}_{M2} = \frac{1}{\lambda_M} \mathbf{\Psi}^{-1}(\vec{\mu} + \mathbf{C}\vec{\pi}), \tag{C.21}$$

and

$$\vec{\mathbf{f}}(\vec{\mathbf{v}}) = \vec{\mathbf{x}}_{M1} - \vec{\mathbf{x}}_{M2}. \tag{C.22}$$

6. New Empirical Evidence for Popularity

It is one thing to look in the past at the well-known premiums and anomalies in connection with a proposed asset pricing model and to find an after-the-fact explanation that seems to hold. It is another thing to see whether the predictions of a new model hold for security characteristics that have not been previously tested in the empirical asset pricing literature. In this chapter, we test the relationship between returns and various measures of characteristics that investors should nearly universally like or dislike. Broadly speaking, these measures can be divided into those that pertain to characteristics of companies and those that pertain to characteristics of the securities that they issue.

In the first section of this chapter, we analyze data on company characteristics that could make a company popular or unpopular. For each characteristic, we see if the stocks of the least popular companies outperform those of the most popular companies. We look at three characteristics that, to our knowledge, have not previously been examined in the literature: brand value, competitive advantage, and company reputation.

In the second section, we look at two stock-level characteristics: severe tail risk, as represented by low or negative coskewness with a market index (a nearly uniformly unpopular characteristic), and lottery-like payoffs (a nearly uniformly popular characteristic).

For each popularity measure, we consider four portfolios formed by dividing the universe of stocks into equally populated quartiles such that Quartile 1 contains the most popular stocks and Quartile 4 contains the least popular stocks. We also follow this convention, where possible, in Chapter 7. Both here and in Chapter 7, our empirical analysis is largely a comparison of the historical performance of the quartile portfolios formed using each popularity measure.

Popular Company Characteristics

Although a single mutually agreed-upon best measure of a security's popularity does not exist, we have identified several previously unstudied characteristics that could serve as proxies for dimensions of popularity. These traits include the value of a brand, the degree to which a company is estimated to have a sustainable competitive advantage, and the reputation of the company. We use the following measures of these dimensions of popularity:

1. Interbrand's annual "Best Global Brands" report—On an annual basis, Interbrand publishes a list of the 100 brands with the highest estimated

"brand value." We tested whether significant performance differences exist among the evolving top 100 brands.

2. Morningstar's economic moat ratings—Morningstar's equity analysts evaluate a number of factors related to a company's relative sustainable competitive advantage (considered a moat to deter competition), including network effect, intangible assets, cost advantage, switching costs, and efficient scale. On the basis of this analysis, they classify each company as having (1) a wide moat, (2) a narrow moat, or (3) no moat. A sustainable competitive advantage is an example of a characteristic that investors would nearly uniformly agree is good.

3. Nielsen's Harris Poll reputation quotient (see Harris Poll 2015)—The Harris Poll reputation quotient measures the reputations of companies in the United States in which *consumers* rate corporations by 20 attributes that are categorized into six dimensions, which ultimately form the reputation quotient. We believe the reputation quotient aligns well with characteristics that investors seek and thus can serve as a proxy for a dimension of popularity. Our analysis is similar to that of Statman, Fisher, and Anginer (2008), who studied *Fortune*'s most admired companies, although the *Fortune* rankings are based on the opinions of senior executives and analysts rather than general consumers.

In the following sections, we present an analysis of the relationship between each of these measures of popularity and returns.

Brand Value. Interbrand was founded in 1974 and is one of the world's largest branding consultancies. Starting in 2000, Interbrand began publishing an annual "Best Global Brands" report.[37] This report identifies and ranks the top global brands based on a proprietary methodology for estimating the net present value (NPV) of a company's earnings related to brand value.[38]

Interbrand's methodology combines financial, demand, and competitor analyses to estimate the NPV of earnings related to brand value. To be included in the Interbrand study, a company must meet a number of criteria; namely, 30% or more of revenue must come from outside the home region and the company must have a presence in at least three continents, have publicly

---

[37]See www.interbrand.com/wp-content/uploads/2018/02/Best-Global-Brands-2017.pdf.
[38]Huang (2015), who compared the primary methodologies for estimating brand value, characterized the Interbrand methodology as an asset-based approach (rather than a customer-based approach or comprehensive approach).

available financials, and have the expectation of positive long-term economic profits.

To estimate the value of a brand, Interbrand starts by estimating the economic profit of the company in question. Economic profit is then multiplied by what Interbrand calls the "role of brand" measure, which attempts to identify the portion of the buying decision attributable to brand. According to the methodology description, the "Role of Brand reflects the portion of demand for a branded retailer that exceeds what the demand would be for the same offering if it were unbranded." Multiplying the estimated economic value by the role of brand leads to what Interbrand calls "brand earnings." To determine the brand value, brand earnings are discounted by a brand-specific discount rate, by which Interbrand evaluates brand strength along 10 dimensions. Although not a perfect measure of popularity, this measure of brand value captures the power of the brand and is thus strongly influenced by brand popularity.

Other researchers have not interpreted brand value as a proxy for popularity, but they have found links between brand value and stock returns, although not in the direction predicted by our popularity theory. For example, using 1,204 brand value estimates for 1991–1996, Barth, Clement, Foster, and Kasznik (1998) found brand value to be positively related to stock prices and returns. Madden, Fehle, and Fournier (2006) and Fehle, Fournier, Madden, and Shrider (2008), after using the three-factor Fama–French model to adjust for risk plus a momentum factor, found that stocks associated with strong brands as measured by Interbrand statistically and economically outperformed.

These observations appear to be inconsistent with the popularity hypothesis, which predicts that stocks with strong brands are popular so they should underperform. The conclusions in Fehle et al. (2008) were drawn from a small sample size (only 111 stocks) and a short period that corresponded with the dot-com euphoria of 1994–2000; thus, the findings may not be robust over time. The August 1994 to December 2000 measurement period study by Fehle et al. could be considered the time of a unique inflating bubble, in which popular stocks became even more popular, with growth and large-capitalization stocks dramatically outperforming. Note also that Portfolio 3 in Table 2 of Fehle et al. was rebalanced annually and each year contained only the companies on the most recent Interbrand list. Hence, it is more relevant than Portfolios 1 and 2. The results for Portfolio 3 are not statistically significant, however, whereas the results for Portfolios 1 and 2 are. Thus, we find their conclusions unconvincing.

We took a different approach from Fehle et al. (2008). Instead of grouping all stocks in the Interbrand list, we studied the cross-sectional performance *differences* among all stocks on that list. Our cross-sectional analyses allowed us to study the impact of changes in brand value over time, and we show that within the Interbrand list, the more popular stocks (higher brand values) underperform the less popular stocks (lower brand values).

Interbrand supplied us with a spreadsheet containing the top brands for each calendar year starting in 2000 and ending in 2017. Much of this information is publicly available, but it is tedious to consolidate in a usable form.[39] In the initial year, 2000, the list contained only 75 brands; the rest of the years contained 100 brands. **Table 6.1** displays the first 50 brands, the brand ranks, and Interbrand's estimated brand value (BV) for 2000 and 2017.

Some observations about the data in Table 6.1 are worth noting. First, the relationship between brands and stocks is not always one to one. To address this issue, in some cases, we mapped brand to publicly traded stocks. In other cases, where multiple brands (such as Volkswagen, Audi, and Porsche) are part of the same company (in this case, the Volkswagen Group), we combined the brand values under the parent company so we could eventually sort the group on the basis of the total brand value of an identified stock. Brands of privately held companies, such as IKEA, were excluded from the study.

The list of brands and stocks associated with them represent companies listed on the New York Stock Exchange (NYSE), Nasdaq Stock Market, and other international exchanges. For stocks from international stock exchanges with American depositary receipts (ADRs), we used the ADR. If an ADR was unavailable, we converted returns from the non-US exchange into US dollar–based returns. We carefully recorded mergers, acquisitions, and spin-offs. Some stocks ranked similarly throughout the study (examples are IBM and GE), whereas others changed dramatically. For example, Google was not even on the list in 2000 but had climbed to #2 by 2017; Nokia was #5 in 2000 but was no longer on the list by 2017. For the year 2000 rankings, we were able to link 51 of the 75 brands to a specific stock. Over time, the number of brands that we could link to unique stocks changed, with 79 brands linked to stocks in the final year of this analysis, 2017.

To study the impact of evolving popularity, starting prior to the first trading date in April of each year, based on the most recent BV ranking at the time (the rankings are released in late September or early October of the

---

[39]http://interbrand.com/best-brands/best-global-brands/2017/ranking/#?listFormat=ls.

Table 6.1. Interbrand's Annual Best Global Brands Top 50: 2000 and 2017

2000 Rank	Brand	Sector	2000 BV	2017 Rank	Brand	Sector	2017 BV
1	Coca-Cola	Beverages	72,537	1	Apple	Technology	184,154
2	Microsoft	Technology	70,196	2	Google	Technology	141,703
3	IBM	Business services	53,183	3	Microsoft	Technology	79,999
4	Intel	Technology	39,048	4	Coca-Cola	Beverages	69,733
5	Nokia	Electronics	38,528	5	Amazon	Retail	64,796
6	GE	Diversified	38,127	6	Samsung	Technology	56,249
7	Ford	Automotive	36,368	7	Toyota	Automotive	50,291
8	Disney	Media	33,553	8	Facebook	Technology	48,188
9	McDonald's	Restaurants	27,859	9	Mercedes-Benz	Automotive	47,829
10	AT&T	Telecoms services	25,548	10	IBM	Business services	46,829
11	Marlboro	Tobacco	22,111	11	GE	Diversified	44,208
12	Mercedes-Benz	Automotive	21,104	12	McDonald's	Restaurants	41,533
13	HP	Technology	20,572	13	BMW	Automotive	41,521
14	Cisco	Business services	20,067	14	Disney	Media	40,772
15	Toyota	Automotive	18,823	15	Intel	Technology	39,459
16	Citi	Financial services	18,809	16	Cisco	Technology	31,930
17	Gillette	FMCG	17,358	17	Oracle	Technology	27,466
18	Sony	Electronics	16,409	18	Nike	Sporting goods	27,021
19	American Express	Financial services	16,122	19	Louis Vuitton	Luxury	22,919
20	Honda	Automotive	15,244	20	Honda	Automotive	22,696
21	Compaq	Technology	14,602	21	SAP	Technology	22,635
22	Nescafe	Beverages	13,680	22	Pepsi	Beverages	20,491
23	BMW	Automotive	12,969	23	H&M	Apparel	20,488
24	Kodak	Electronics	11,822	24	Zara	Apparel	18,573
25	Heinz	FMCG	11,742	25	IKEA	Retail	18,472
26	Budweiser	Alcohol	10,684	26	Gillette	FMCG	18,200
27	Xerox	Technology	9,699	27	American Express	Financial services	17,787
28	Dell	Technology	9,476	28	Pampers	FMCG	16,416

(continued)

Table 6.1.   Interbrand's Annual Best Global Brands Top 50: 2000 and 2017 (continued)

2000 Rank	Brand	Sector	2000 BV	2017 Rank	Brand	Sector	2017 BV
29	Gap	Apparel	9,316	29	UPS	Logistics	16,387
30	Nike	Sporting goods	8,015	30	J.P. Morgan	Financial services	15,749
31	Volkswagen	Automotive	7,834	31	Budweiser	Alcohol	15,375
32	Ericsson	Electronics	7,805	32	Hermès	Luxury	14,210
33	Kellogg's	FMCG	7,357	33	Ford	Automotive	13,643
34	Louis Vuitton	Luxury	6,887	34	eBay	Retail	13,224
35	Pepsi	Beverages	6,637	35	Hyundai	Automotive	13,193
36	Apple	Technology	6,594	36	Nescafe	Beverages	12,661
37	MTV	Media	6,411	37	Accenture	Business services	12,471
38	Yahoo!	Internet services	6,299	38	Audi	Automotive	12,023
39	SAP	Business services	6,135	39	Nissan	Automotive	11,534
40	IKEA	Home furnishings	6,031	40	Volkswagen	Automotive	11,522
41	Duracell	FMCG	5,885	41	Philips	Electronics	11,519
42	Philips	Electronics	5,481	42	AXA	Financial services	11,073
43	Samsung	Technology	5,223	43	Kellogg's	FMCG	10,972
44	Gucci	Luxury	5,149	44	Goldman Sachs	Financial services	10,864
45	Kleenex	FMCG	5,144	45	L'Oréal	FMCG	10,674
46	Reuters	Media	4,876	46	Citi	Financial services	10,599
47	AOL	Internet services	4,531	47	HSBC	Financial services	10,534
48	Amazon	Internet services	4,528	48	Porsche	Automotive	10,129
49	Motorola	Electronics	4,445	49	Allianz	Financial services	10,059
50	Colgate	FMCG	4,417	50	Siemens	Diversified	9,982

Note: FMCG stands for fast moving consumer goods.

previous year), we linked brands to specific stocks. If multiple brands in the rankings were associated with a single stock, then prior to ranking the stocks, we summed the various brands belonging to the single company to arrive at an aggregate value for a given stock. We used those values as the basis of the ranking.

We then divided the stocks into quartiles based on their associated brands. Each quartile contains the same number of constituents plus or minus one stock. We equally weighted the returns on the stocks within each quartile. If a company was acquired by another company, we removed the stock of the acquired company from the sample as of the month of the acquisition, which could cause the number of stocks in a quartile to temporarily be lower than the other quartiles. Quartile 1 consists of the 25% of stocks with the highest BV (51 possible stocks divided into quartiles resulted in approximately 13 stocks in 2000, and 79 stocks divided into quartiles resulted in approximately 20 stocks per quartile in 2017). Quartile 4 consists of the 25% of stocks with the lowest BV.

In this and the next section, we report portfolio performance as measured against both equally weighted and market cap–weighted benchmarks. We rebalanced equally weighted portfolios back to equal weights at the beginning of each month. Cap-weighted portfolio weights were based on market-cap values at the beginning of each month. Note that equally weighted portfolios tended to have better performance than cap-weighted portfolios because of the rebalancing premium.[40] Therefore, we used equally weighted portfolios as benchmarks for equally weighted portfolios in computing Jensen's alpha (Jensen 1968) and used the Carhart four factors (Carhart 1997) to compute the Carhart alpha for cap-weighted portfolios because the Carhart four factors are cap weighted.[41]

Table 6.2 presents summary statistics for the annually constituted (with monthly rebalancing back to equal weights) BV-based quartiles.

Focusing initially on annual geometric returns, we see when we move from left to right, from Quartile 4 (Q4) containing the stocks with the lowest BV (least popular stocks) to Quartile 1 (Q1) containing the stocks with the

---

[40]Plyakha, Uppal, and Vilkov (2014) showed that with monthly rebalancing, an equal-weighted portfolio outperforms a value-weighted portfolio in terms of total mean return, four-factor alpha, and Sharpe ratio. They explained that this outperformance is partly because the equal-weighted portfolio has higher exposure to systematic risk factors (size and value), but a considerable part (42%) of the outperformance comes from the difference in alphas, which is a consequence of the rebalancing to maintain constant weights in the equal-weighted portfolio. The existence of a "pure" rebalancing premium (one not related to size or value) is not universally agreed upon; see Huss and Maloney (2017).

[41]The Carhart four factors are the three Fama–French factors plus a momentum factor.

Table 6.2.   **Summary Statistics of Equally Weighted Quartile Returns Based on Interbrand's Global Brand Value (BV) Rankings, April 2000–August 2017**

Measure	Quartile 4 (lowest BV)	Quartile 3	Quartile 2	Quartile 1 (highest BV)
Geometric mean (%)	11.95	8.85	7.61	5.87
Arithmetic mean (%)	13.53	10.89	8.95	7.39
Standard deviation (%)	16.73	19.30	15.87	16.90
Sharpe ratio	0.705	0.476	0.459	0.340
Skewness	−0.556	−0.312	−0.076	−0.376
Jensen's alpha (%)	3.50	−0.62	−0.32	−2.47
t-stat. of alpha	2.30	−0.44	−0.24	−2.04

highest BV (most popular stocks) that the lower-BV quartiles monotonically outperformed the higher-BV quartiles. The same monotonic relationship holds for the Sharpe ratio: Q4 has a significantly higher Sharpe ratio than the other three quartiles. We found no consistent relationship for standard deviation across the quartiles.

The last two rows of Table 6.2 show Jensen's annualized alpha and the corresponding t-statistic for each quartile.[42] We used the equally weighted portfolios for all stocks across the quartiles as the benchmark and ran simple regressions to get Jensen's annualized alphas. Note the wide differences in Jensen's alpha (and t-statistics) for the first and fourth quartiles.

Figure 6.1 shows the growth of a $1 investment in each of the quartiles on a logarithmic scale, which allows a comparison of return changes through time. Here, we see that the monotonic performance relationship captured by the summary statistics in Table 6.2 has not always held in the growth of $1 race.

Table 6.3 presents various performance summary statistics for the cap-weighted four quartiles. The last two rows show the alphas against the Carhart four factors. The results are generally consistent with Table 6.2, but the t-statistics are less significant.

Overall, based on brand, both the equally weighted composites and cap-weighted composites are consistent with the popularity thesis and are in contrast to the risk–return paradigm.

---

[42]Jensen's alpha is the intercept from a regression of the portfolio's return (in excess of the riskless rate) on the return of a market index or some other appropriately selected benchmark (again, in excess of the riskless rate). The use of regression to perform the calculation properly accounts for any potential difference in betas (market-related risks) of the two variables (the portfolio excess return and the market index or benchmark excess return).

Figure 6.1. Growth of $1 for Equally Weighted Quartiles Based on Interbrand's BV Rankings, April 2000–August 2017 (log scale)

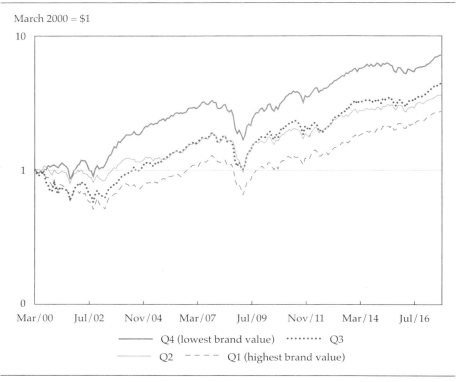

March 2000 = $1

Legend:
— Q4 (lowest brand value) ·········· Q3
— Q2 – – – – Q1 (highest brand value)

Table 6.3. Summary Statistics of Cap-Weighted Quartile Returns Based on Interbrand's BV Rankings, April 2000–August 2017

Measure	Q4 (lowest BV)	Q3	Q2	Q1 (highest BV)
Geometric mean (%)	7.27	5.00	3.12	3.79
Arithmetic mean (%)	8.30	7.02	4.48	5.40
Standard deviation (%)	13.85	19.38	16.18	17.50
Sharpe ratio	0.479	0.277	0.178	0.216
Skewness	−0.626	−0.624	−0.352	−0.401
Carhart's alpha (%)	2.58	0.66	−1.12	1.02
t-stat. of alpha	1.52	0.31	−0.61	0.58

Competitive Advantage. Morningstar's economic moat idea is an estimate of a company's sustainable competitive advantage—a characteristic that investors nearly uniformly agree is good. To calculate economic moats, Morningstar's equity analysts evaluate and estimate a company's sustainable competitive advantage on the basis of five criteria: network effect, intangible assets, cost advantage, switching costs, and efficient scale. Based on the equity analysts' assessment of each company with respect to one or more of these criteria, each company is given a rating of wide moat, narrow moat, or no moat. Morningstar started assigning moat ratings in 2002. The economic moat idea measures the quality of a *business* and has nothing to do with whether or not the security in question is priced fairly.

The period of our analysis of economic moat and returns is July 2002 through August 2017. The number of companies that had economic moat ratings in our sample varied over time—with a minimum of 427 (July 2002), a maximum of 1,611 (November 2008), and an average of 1,039 companies. **Figure 6.2** shows the distribution of economic moat ratings through time. Note that the number of stocks for each of the three moat ratings is not the same.

Starting in July 2002, we placed each stock in the universe of moat-rated stocks into three groups, based on their moat ratings. We updated the three ratings groups each month on the basis of the most recent publicly available moat ratings. We believe that investors prefer companies they consider to have a sustainable competitive advantage. Thus, wide-moat companies represent the most popular stocks and no-moat companies represent the least popular stocks. **Table 6.4** presents various performance summary statistics for the equally weighted portfolios corresponding to the three moat ratings.

In Table 6.4, as we move from no-moat companies with, on average, the lowest sustainable competitive advantage (least popular companies) to the wide-moat companies with, on average, the highest sustainable competitive advantage (most unpopular companies), we find that the no-moat companies produced the most superior arithmetic and geometric mean returns. This additional return came, however, with more risk.

The last two rows of Table 6.4 show Jensen's annualized alpha and its *t*-statistic. We used the equally weighted returns for all stocks across the three moat ratings as the market return and ran simple regressions to get Jensen's annualized alpha. The annualized alphas are –1.59% for the no-moat companies and 0.95% for the wide-moat companies, which is the opposite of what one might expect given that no-moat companies had a much higher geometric return than wide-moat companies. Neither of the alphas is statistically significant at the 5% level.

Figure 6.2. Distribution of Economic Moat Ratings, July 2002–August 2017

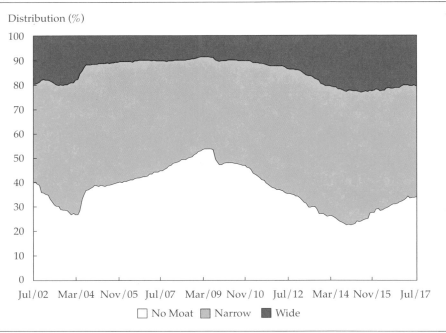

Figure 6.3 shows the growth of a $1 investment for each of the three moat ratings. For this historical period, in up markets, the lower the sustainable competitive advantage, the better the returns. During down markets, however, such as the 2008 financial crisis and the more minor downturns in 2011 and 2015, the greater the sustainable competitive advantage, the milder the downturn.

Table 6.4. Summary Statistics for Equally Weighted Portfolios Based on Morningstar's Economic Moat Ratings, July 2002–August 2017

Measure	No Moat	Narrow Moat	Wide Moat
Geometric mean (%)	15.40	12.08	11.15
Arithmetic mean (%)	18.57	13.52	12.13
Standard deviation (%)	23.59	16.08	13.26
Sharpe ratio	0.729	0.758	0.815
Skewness	0.169	−0.400	−0.565
Jensen's alpha (%)	−1.59	−0.28	0.95
t-stat. of alpha	−1.11	−0.52	1.21

Figure 6.3. Growth of $1 for the Three Equally Weighted Portfolios Based on Morningstar Economic Moat Ratings, July 2002–August 2017 (log scale)

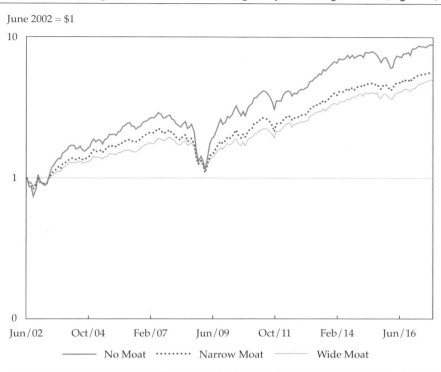

June 2002 = $1

——— No Moat · · · · · · · · Narrow Moat ——— Wide Moat

Table 6.5 presents various performance summary statistics for the cap-weighted portfolios based on the three moat ratings. The last two rows show the alphas against the Carhart four factors. In general, the results in Table 6.5 are consistent with those in Table 6.4.

Overall, based on competitive advantage, both the equally weighted composites and cap-weighted composites are consistent with *both* the popularity and the risk–return paradigms. The composites with no competitive advantage (unpopular stocks) produced the highest geometric returns but did so with the highest amount of risk.

Reputation. First introduced in 1999, the Harris Poll reputation quotient (Harris Poll 2015) has used a consistent methodology to measure the "reputation" of the most visible US companies for the last 15 years. The Harris Poll study involves two phases. It starts with a "nomination phase" in which the general public is asked to identify the US companies with the best and worst reputations. In this phase, 100 companies with the highest or best

Table 6.5. **Summary Statistics for the Cap-Weighted Portfolios Based on Morningstar's Economic Moat Ratings, July 2002–August 2017**

Measure	No Moat	Narrow Moat	Wide Moat
Geometric mean (%)	9.94	9.88	8.37
Arithmetic mean (%)	12.13	11.14	9.20
Standard deviation (%)	19.76	15.10	12.40
Sharpe ratio	0.548	0.652	0.639
Skewness	−0.669	−0.745	−0.563
Carhart's alpha (%)	−0.47	0.71	0.75
t-stat. of alpha	−0.39	1.13	0.85

reputations are identified. Prior to 2015, only the 60 best companies were identified. For the 2015 study, 4,034 interviews were conducted to identify the top 100 companies. In the second phase, the "rating phase," on the basis of a 20-minute interview (with approximately 250 adults participating in the interviews), each of the companies is rated on 20 attributes (classified into six categories). We treated the Harris Poll reputation quotient as a proxy for a dimension of popularity.

The Harris Poll reputation quotient (RQ) is most similar in spirit to *Fortune*'s most admired companies, although rather than polling the general public, the *Fortune* survey polls senior executives, directors, and securities analysts when identifying the most admired companies. The Harris Poll RQ may also seem similar to Interbrand's BV rankings, but the Harris Poll is survey based and focuses on reputation, whereas the Interbrand rankings are valuation based and focus on estimated brand value. Thus, the two ranking organizations are measuring two distinct characteristics of a company.

In contrast to Interbrand BV ranks, in which multiple brands from a single company may appear on their list, the Harris Poll collapses subsidiaries and brands into a single parent company. As in previous analyses, we manually linked each publicly traded company to an appropriate stock ticker and removed privately held companies. We linked the Harris Poll RQ to tickers on the NYSE and NASDAQ and to ADRs.

Table 6.6 shows the top-ranked RQ companies, their rank, and their RQs for the first year of the poll (2000) and the 2017 poll. The constituents and the rank orders have changed substantially over time.

Mirroring the process that we applied to the Interbrand brand values, we used RQ ranks to form quartiles. The updated annual RQ ranks are typically released in February; thus, we delayed quartile formation until April of each year. Again, Quartile 1 contains the 25% of companies with the highest RQs

Table 6.6. Harris Poll RQ Top 40 for 2000 and Top 50 for 2017

	2000			2017	
Rank	Company Name	RQ Score	Rank	Company Name	RQ Score
1	Johnson & Johnson	83.4	1	Amazon.com	86.3
2	Coca-Cola Co.	81.6	2	Wegman's Food Markets	85.4
3	Hewlett-Packard Co.	81.2	3	SpaceX	83.1
4	Ben & Jerry's Ice Cream	81.0	4	Publix Supermarkets	82.8
5	Intel Corp.	81.0	5	Johnson & Johnson	82.6
6	Walmart	80.5	6	Apple	82.1
7	Xerox	79.9	7	UPS	82.1
8	Home Depot	79.7	8	Walt Disney Co.	82.0
9	Gateway	78.8	9	Google	82.0
10	Walt Disney Co.	78.7	10	Tesla Motors	81.7
11	Dell	78.4	11	3M Co.	81.5
12	General Electric	78.1	12	USAA	81.4
13	Anheuser-Busch	78.0	13	Alphabet Inc.	81.3
14	Lucent Technologies	78.0	14	Coca-Cola Co.	81.2
15	Microsoft	77.9	15	General Mills	81.2
16	Amazon	77.8	16	Costco	81.1
17	IBM	77.6	17	Clorox Co.	81.1
18	Sony	77.4	18	Under Armour	80.7
19	Yahoo!	76.9	19	Toyota Motor Corp.	80.2
20	FedEx Corp.	75.7	20	L.L. Bean	80.1
21	AT&T	75.7	21	Netflix	79.9
22	Procter & Gamble Co.	71.9	22	SC Johnson	79.7
23	Nike	71.3	23	Lowe's	79.7
24	McDonald's	71.2	24	Microsoft	79.3
25	Southwest Airlines	70.6	25	Kroger Co.	79.2
26	AOL	69.2	26	Berkshire Hathaway	79.2
27	Fiat Chrysler Automobiles	69.1	27	PayPal	79.0
28	Toyota Motor Corp.	68.6	28	FedEx Corp.	79.0
29	Sears Holdings Corp.	67.6	29	Kimberly-Clark Corp.	78.9
30	Boeing Co.	67.3	30	LG Corp.	78.8
31	Texaco	67.3	31	Boeing Co.	78.7

(continued)

Table 6.6.   Harris Poll RQ Top 40 for 2000 and Top 50 for 2017 (continued)

	2000			2017	
Rank	Company Name	RQ Score	Rank	Company Name	RQ Score
32	Ford Motor Co.	66.9	32	Meijer's	78.7
33	General Motors	63.1	33	Southwest Airlines	78.6
34	Apple	62.1	34	Chick-fil-A	78.5
35	MCI/WorldCom	62	35	BMW	78.2
36	ExxonMobil	61.6	36	Vanguard Group	78.2
37	Kmart	60.5	37	Nestle	78.1
38	Bank of America	58.8	38	Whirlpool Corp.	78.0
39	Amway	58.1	39	General Electric	77.9
40	Philip Morris Companies	57.2	40	Prosper	77.9
			41	Hewlett-Packard Co.	77.8
			42	Honda Motor Co.	77.8
			43	Subaru	77.6
			44	Kellogg Co.	77.6
			45	Hobby Lobby	77.5
			46	Nike	77.5
			47	Visa	77.3
			48	Whole Foods Market	77.2
			49	Mondelez International	77.1
			50	Walgreens	77.1

(the most popular companies) and Quartile 4 contains the 25% of companies with the lowest RQs (the least popular companies).

Table 6.7 and **Figure 6.4** present, respectively, summary statistics and the growth of a $1 investment in each RQ quartile.

In Table 6.7, we see as we move from Q4 containing the stocks with the lowest RQs (most unpopular stocks) through the various quartiles to Q1 containing the stocks with the highest RQs (most popular stocks) that the lower-RQ quartiles outperformed the higher-RQ quartiles on the basis of arithmetic return. Q4 with the lowest RQs had a significantly better geometric return and Sharpe ratio than the other quartiles, but Q4 also had the highest standard deviation.

Table 6.7. Summary Statistics of Equally Weighted Quartile Portfolios Based on Harris Poll RQ Rankings, April 2000–August 2017

Measure	Q4 (lowest RQ value)	Q3	Q2	Q1 (highest RQ value)
Geometric mean (%)	12.61	7.14	5.66	7.02
Arithmetic mean (%)	14.73	8.97	7.50	8.41
Standard deviation (%)	19.51	18.56	18.56	16.10
Sharpe ratio	0.665	0.393	0.315	0.418
Skewness	−0.038	0.122	−0.413	−0.344
Jensen's alpha (%)	4.01	−1.09	−2.56	−0.25
t-stat. of alpha	1.88	−0.65	−1.67	−0.16

Figure 6.4. Growth of $1 for the Equally Weighted Quartile Portfolios Based on Harris Poll RQs, April 2000–August 2017 (log scale)

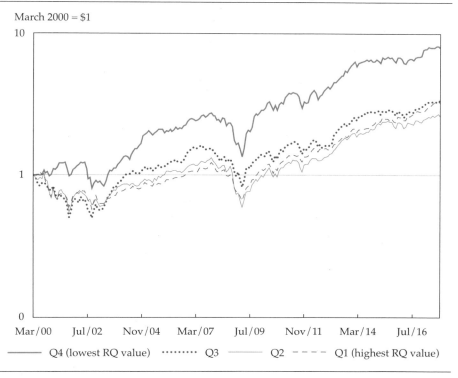

The annual return differences in Table 6.7 are qualitatively and quantitatively similar to the results reported in Statman et al. (2008), who studied *Fortune*'s most admired companies between September 1982 and September 2006, although Statman et al. split the stocks into two groups ("spurned" and "admired") rather than quartiles and varied the reconstitution time period.

The last two rows in Table 6.7 show Jensen's annualized alpha and its *t*-statistic. We used the equally weighted returns for all stocks across the quartiles as the benchmark and ran simple regressions to get Jensen's annualized alpha. The annualized alphas for the lowest and highest poll values are far apart.

Figure 6.4 shows the superior performance of Quartile 4, stocks with the lowest RQ.

Table 6.8 presents various performance summary statistics for the cap-weighted four quartiles. The last two rows show the alphas against the Carhart four factors. Overall, the results are consistent with Table 6.7. A difference is that Carhart's alpha for Q1 is the highest ($\alpha = 3.80\%$). A close look shows that Q1 is loaded with a negative HML (high book/market minus low book/market, the value factor) coefficient ($\beta = -0.32$, *t*-statistic $= -6.40$) and negative momentum coefficient ($\beta = -0.09$, *t*-statistic $= -2.98$), and Q4 is loaded with a positive HML coefficient ($\beta = 0.39$, *t*-statistic $= 7.28$) and positive momentum coefficient ($\beta = 0.01$, *t*-statistic $= 0.37$). The other two factor loadings ($R_m - R_f$ and SMB, or small minus big, the size factor) are similar for Q1 and Q4. Q4 is apparently capturing some value effect, which is consistent with the notion that a previously popular company moves toward being a value company when it is getting less popular and a previously unpopular company moves toward being a growth company when it is getting more popular.

Overall, based on company reputation, the equally weighted composites are consistent with both popularity and the risk–return paradigm. However,

Table 6.8. Summary Statistics of Cap-Weighted Quartile Portfolios Based on Harris Poll RQ Rankings, April 2000–August 2017

Measure	Q4 (lowest poll value)	Q3	Q2	Q1 (highest poll value)
Geometric mean (%)	8.49	−0.07	3.41	6.07
Arithmetic mean (%)	9.74	1.25	4.86	7.37
Standard deviation (%)	15.18	16.03	16.59	15.58
Sharpe ratio	0.532	−0.018	0.196	0.367
Skewness	−0.303	−0.607	−0.551	−0.572
Carhart's alpha (%)	2.91	−3.74	−0.72	3.80
t-stat. of alpha	1.46	−1.71	−0.41	2.04

the cap-weighted composites are not monotonic, and in our judgment, they are moderately consistent with the popularity theory but lack a clear relationship between return and risk. Given the relatively small number of companies in the composites, the market-cap composites may be heavily influenced by a small number of stocks. For both the equally weighted and market-cap weighted composites, the quartiles with the worst company reputations (unpopular stocks) produced the highest geometric returns.

Tail Risk (Coskewness)

Kraus and Litzenberger (1976) showed that investors dislike stocks with returns with high tail risk as measured by negative coskewness with the market. Thus, stocks with more negative coskewness tend to have higher expected returns. Negative coskewness means that the security in question contributes negatively to the skewness of the market portfolio, so the security is expected to experience large losses when the market falls. Harvey and Siddique (2000) suggested that the stocks with negative coskewness should command a higher expected return than those with positive coskewness because negatively skewed returns are less desirable.[43] Indeed, by studying past returns, the authors showed that coskewness has been economically important and has earned a risk premium of, on average, 3.6% per year for US stocks.

In this section, we report empirical analyses similar to those of Harvey and Siddique (2000) but focused on the subsequent 20-year period—basically an out-of-sample test of their analysis.[44]

Starting in January 1991 and using the first 60 months of returns, we sorted the universe of all US stocks from lowest or most negative coskewness (least popular) to highest or most positive coskewness (most popular), and we assigned companies to one of four quartiles. We averaged monthly returns starting from January 1996 with equal weights for each quartile. We updated the quartiles monthly.

---

[43]Harvey and Siddique (2000) defined the standardized unconditional coskewness as

$\text{Coskewness} = \left[E(\varepsilon_{i,t} \varepsilon_{M,t}^2) \right] / \sqrt{E(\varepsilon_{i,t}^2)} E(\varepsilon_{M,t}^2)$, where $\varepsilon_{i,t} = r_{i,t} - r_{ft} - \beta_i (r_{M,t} - r_{ft})$

and $\varepsilon_{m,t} = r_{M,t} - \text{avg}(r_{M,t})$.

The residual ($\varepsilon_{i,t}$) is computed from the regression of the excess return on the contemporaneous market excess return for security i in period t. The term $\varepsilon_{m,t}$ is the market return in period t in excess of average market return.

[44]Our data consist of the stock universe consisting of all the stocks on the NYSE, American Stock Exchange, and NASDAQ for the 26-year period from January 1991 through August 2017. We collected monthly returns from Morningstar Direct. We included stocks with an initial price greater than $5 in each period. We excluded derivative securities of foreign stocks, such as ADRs. January 1991 covers 833 stocks, and August 2017 covers 2,219 stocks.

Table 6.9 presents various performance summary statistics for the equally weighted quartiles. Quartile 4 consists primarily of the lowest, or most negative, coskewness companies, and Quartile 1 consists of the highest, or most positive, coskewness companies. We believe that investors prefer companies that have high positive coskewness. Thus, along this dimension of popularity, Q1 represents the most popular stocks and Q4 represents the least popular.

In Table 6.9, as we move from left to right from Q4 of companies with the lowest or most negative coskewness (least popular companies) to Q1 of companies with the highest or most positive coskewness (most popular companies), we see that companies with lower coskewness monotonically produced superior arithmetic and geometric mean returns. This additional return came with nearly equal standard deviations (inferring no relationship between risk and return), so the Sharpe ratios are monotonically decreasing from Q4 to Q1. Table 6.9 thus confirms the empirical findings of Harvey and Siddique (2000) in an out-of-sample sense.

The annualized Jensen's alphas for Q1 and Q4, both statistically significant at the 5% level, support the popularity thesis.

Figure 6.5 shows the growth of a $1 investment in each of the four quartiles. The lowest coskewness portfolio outperformed the highest coskewness portfolio.

Table 6.10 presents various summary performance statistics for the cap-weighted four quartiles. The last two rows show the alphas against the Carhart four factors. In general, the results are consistent with Table 6.9, but the *t*-statistics are less significant.

Table 6.9. Summary Statistics of Equally Weighted Quartile Portfolios Based on Coskewness, January 1996–August 2017

Measure	Q4 (most negative coskewness)	Q3	Q2	Q1 (least negative or most positive coskewness)
Geometric mean (%)	12.16	9.67	9.57	8.21
Arithmetic mean (%)	13.39	10.85	10.79	9.39
Standard deviation (%)	14.74	14.59	14.87	14.75
Sharpe ratio	0.741	0.579	0.564	0.476
Skewness	−0.611	−0.672	−0.638	−0.572
Jensen's alpha (%)	2.22	−0.22	−0.47	−1.49
t-stat. of alpha	2.84	−0.60	−1.23	−2.23

Figure 6.5. **Growth of $1 for Equally Weighted Quartile Portfolios Based on Coskewness, January 1996–August 2017 (log scale)**

December 1995 = $1

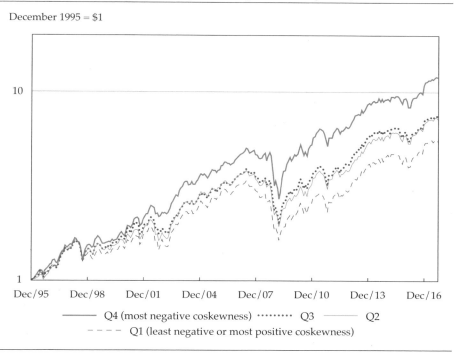

———— Q4 (most negative coskewness) ·········· Q3 ———— Q2
– – – – Q1 (least negative or most positive coskewness)

Table 6.10. **Summary Statistics of Cap-Weighted Quartile Portfolios Based on Coskewness, January 1996–August 2017**

Measure	Q4 (most negative coskewness)	Q3	Q2	Q1 (least negative or most positive coskewness)
Geometric mean (%)	10.83	8.10	8.57	6.15
Arithmetic mean (%)	12.09	9.23	9.78	7.38
Standard deviation (%)	15.04	14.40	14.86	15.18
Sharpe ratio	0.644	0.477	0.498	0.333
Skewness	−0.638	−0.569	−0.715	−0.527
Carhart's alpha (%)	2.43	−0.16	0.18	−1.70
t-stat. of alpha	1.86	−0.16	0.18	−1.72

Overall, based on coskewness, both the equally weighted composites and cap-weighted composites are consistent with popularity and are inconsistent with the risk–return paradigm.

Lottery Stocks

A number of empirical studies have shown that portfolios held by individual investors are often underdiversified, containing fewer than five stocks, on average. Example studies are Odean (1999), Mitton and Vorkink (2007), Kumar (2007), and Goetzmann and Kumar (2008). Statman (2004) called the situation the "diversification puzzle" because this underdiversification choice is inconsistent with portfolio theory—that is, by the simple act of diversifying, investors should be able to obtain an equivalent expected return at a much lower expected standard deviation or, conversely, a much higher expected return at an equivalent expected standard deviation.

The key to understanding this puzzle is investors' preferences for positive skewness, as described by Xiong and Idzorek (forthcoming 2019). A considerable body of empirical evidence shows that individual investors prefer lottery-like stocks (see, for example, Barberis and Huang 2008). Lottery-like stocks have a relatively small probability of a large payoff. From a popularity perspective, this strong preference for lottery-like stocks suggests that lottery-like stocks are *popular*. Indeed, Mitton and Vorkink (2007) found that lottery-like stocks are relatively popular with underdiversified investors.

No single definition of what represents a lottery-like stock or company is accepted. Bali, Cakici, and Whitelaw (2011) used the maximum daily return over the past month as a proxy for lottery stocks. They performed portfolio-level analyses and company-level cross-sectional regressions that showed a negative and significant relationship between the maximum daily return over the past one month (MAX) and expected stock returns. Average raw and risk-adjusted return differences between stocks in the lowest and highest MAX deciles exceeded 1% per month. These results were robust to controls for size, value, momentum, short-term reversals, liquidity, and skewness. This evidence suggests that investors are willing to pay more for stocks that exhibit extreme positive returns; thus, these stocks exhibit lower returns in the future.

For our analysis, we once again formed quartiles on the basis of a proxy for a dimension of popularity—in this case, the strong preference for lottery-like payoffs. We used the same stock universe as we did in the section on tail risk (coskewness). We also used the measure of lottery-like behavior of stocks presented in Bali et al. (2011)—that is, the average return associated with the five best days during the prior month. Starting in January 1991, we formed quartile portfolios every month from February 1991 to August 2017 by sorting stocks on the basis of the average return associated with each stock's five best days during the prior month (MAX-5). Quartile 4 is the portfolio of stocks with the lowest MAX-5 over the past one month (the least popular stocks). Conversely, Quartile 1 is the portfolio of stocks with the highest MAX-5 over the past one month (the most popular stocks).

Consistent with our prior analyses, **Table 6.11** presents summary performance statistics for the four quartiles sorted on MAX-5.

In Table 6.11, moving from left to right from Q4, stocks with the lowest MAX-5 (least popular stocks), to Q1, stocks with the highest MAX-5 (most popular stocks), we see that stocks with lower MAX-5 ratings monotonically produced superior Sharpe ratios. The monotonic increase in standard deviation is also clearly seen across the quartiles, and the highest MAX-5 quartile has the highest volatility. This finding is consistent with the well-known low-volatility anomaly, in that the least popular stocks have the lowest volatility. It indicates that high-volatility stocks have lottery-like payoffs, so they underperform low-volatility stocks *on a risk-adjusted basis*. The widely separated annualized Jensen's alphas for Q4 and Q1 are statistically significant at the 5% level. Our results confirm the results of Bali et al. (2011) on a risk-adjusted basis, although our result for the arithmetic mean return for the lowest MAX-5 quartile is lower than that for the highest MAX-5 quartile.

Figure 6.6 shows the growth of a $1 investment in each of the four quartiles. So, contrary to the popularity hypothesis, the highest MAX-5 daily return portfolio outperformed the lowest MAX-5 daily return portfolio, even though the predictions of the popularity hypothesis do hold up on a risk-adjusted basis.

Table 6.11. Equally Weighted Quartile Summary Statistics Based on the Average of MAX-5 Daily Returns, February 1991–August 2017

Measure	Q4 (lowest MAX-5 daily returns)	Q3	Q2	Q1 (highest MAX-5 daily returns)
Geometric mean (%)	11.63	12.53	12.16	13.35
Arithmetic mean (%)	12.18	13.67	13.95	17.38
Standard deviation (%)	9.98	14.17	17.74	26.67
Sharpe ratio	0.937	0.763	0.625	0.541
Skewness	−0.970	−0.832	−0.617	0.061
Jensen's alpha (%)	4.42	1.73	−1.53	−4.42
t-stat. of alpha	4.38	1.87	−3.67	−2.29

105

Figure 6.6. Growth of $1 for Equally Weighted Quartile Portfolios Based on Average of MAX-5 Daily Returns, February 1991–August 2017 (log scale)

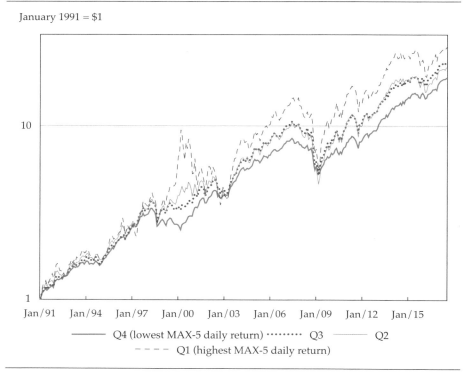

January 1991 = $1

——— Q4 (lowest MAX-5 daily return) ·········· Q3 ——— Q2
– – – – Q1 (highest MAX-5 daily return)

Table 6.12. Summary Statistics for Cap-Weighted Quartile Portfolios Based on the Average of MAX-5 Daily Returns, February 1991–August 2017

Measure	Q4 (lowest MAX-5 daily returns)	Q3	Q2	Q1 (highest MAX-5 daily returns)
Geometric mean (%)	9.46	9.26	10.32	8.40
Arithmetic mean (%)	10.16	10.3	12.21	12.69
Standard deviation (%)	11.26	14.24	18.42	27.73
Sharpe ratio	0.656	0.534	0.510	0.356
Skewness	−0.651	−0.465	−0.491	−0.310
Carhart's alpha (%)	0.53	−0.62	−0.60	−2.00
t-stat. of alpha	0.53	−0.70	−0.57	−0.85

Table 6.12 presents various summary statistics for the market cap–weighted four quartiles. The last two rows show the alphas for the Carhart four factors. Overall, the results are consistent with those presented in Table 6.11, but the *t*-statistics are lower, indicating less statistical significance.

Overall, based on lottery-like stocks (sorts on average of MAX-5 daily returns), the equally weighted composites and cap-weighted composites are consistent with both popularity and the risk–return paradigm; the less popular quartiles monotonically produced better Sharpe ratios, yet higher returns always came with more risk.

Conclusion

In **Table 6.13,** we have consolidated the previous analyses and our assessment of how the results are or are not consistent with the popularity framework and/or risk–return paradigm. We found 10 out of 10 of the analyses to be at least somewhat consistent with the popularity framework, while 5 out of 10 are consistent with the more-risk/more-return paradigm.

Table 6.13. Summary Results and Consistency with Asset Pricing Framework

Characteristic	Statistic	Least Popular Q4	Q3	Q2	Most Popular Q1	Consistent with Popularity	Consistent with More Risk/More Return
Brand							
Equal weighting (4/2000–8/2017)	Geometric mean (%)	11.95	8.85	7.61	5.87	Yes	No
	Arithmetic mean (%)	13.53	10.89	8.95	7.39		
	Standard dev. (%)	16.73	19.30	15.87	16.90		
	Sharpe ratio	0.705	0.476	0.459	0.34		
Market-cap weighting (4/2000–8/2017)	Geometric mean (%)	7.27	5.00	3.12	3.79	Yes	No
	Arithmetic mean (%)	8.30	7.02	4.48	5.40		
	Standard dev. (%)	13.85	19.38	16.18	17.50		
	Sharpe ratio	0.479	0.277	0.178	0.216		

(continued)

Table 6.13. Summary Results and Consistency with Asset Pricing Framework (continued)

Characteristic	Statistic	Least Popular Q4	Q3	Q2	Most Popular Q1	Consistent with Popularity	Consistent with More Risk/More Return
Competitive sustainable advantage		No Moat	Narrow Moat		Wide Moat		
Equal weighting (7/2002–8/2017)	Geometric mean (%)	15.40	12.08		11.15	Yes	Yes
	Arithmetic mean (%)	18.57	13.52		12.13		
	Standard dev. (%)	23.59	16.08		13.26		
	Sharpe ratio	0.729	0.758		0.815		
Market-cap weighting (7/2002–8/2017)	Geometric mean (%)	9.94	9.88		8.37	Yes	Yes
	Arithmetic mean (%)	12.13	11.14		9.20		
	Standard dev. (%)	19.76	15.10		12.40		
	Sharpe ratio	0.548	0.652		0.639		
Company reputation							
Equal weighting (4/2000–8/2017)	Geometric mean (%)	12.61	7.14	5.66	7.02	Yes	Yes
	Arithmetic mean (%)	14.73	8.97	7.50	8.41		
	Standard dev. (%)	19.51	18.56	18.56	16.10		
	Sharpe ratio	0.665	0.393	0.315	0.418		
Market-cap weighting (4/2000–8/2017)	Geometric mean (%)	8.49	−0.07	3.41	6.07	Mixed	No
	Arithmetic mean (%)	9.74	1.25	4.86	7.37		
	Standard dev. (%)	15.18	16.03	16.59	15.58		
	Sharpe ratio	0.532	−0.018	0.196	0.367		

(continued)

Table 6.13. Summary Results and Consistency with Asset Pricing Framework (continued)

Characteristic	Statistic	Least Popular Q4	Q3	Q2	Most Popular Q1	Consistent with Popularity	Consistent with More Risk/More Return
Tail risk (coskewness)							
Equal weighting (1/1996–8/2017)	Geometric mean (%)	12.16	9.67	9.57	8.21	Yes	No
	Arithmetic mean (%)	13.39	10.85	10.79	9.39		
	Standard dev. (%)	14.74	14.59	14.87	14.75		
	Sharpe ratio	0.741	0.579	0.564	0.476		
Market-cap weighting (1/1996–8/2017)	Geometric mean (%)	10.83	8.10	8.57	6.15	Yes	No
	Arithmetic mean (%)	12.09	9.23	9.78	7.38		
	Standard dev. (%)	15.04	14.40	14.86	15.18		
	Sharpe ratio	0.644	0.477	0.498	0.333		
Lottery stocks							
Equal weighting (2/1991–8/2017)	Geometric mean (%)	11.63	12.53	12.16	13.35	Mixed	Mixed
	Arithmetic mean (%)	12.18	13.67	13.95	17.38		
	Standard dev. (%)	9.98	14.17	17.74	26.67		
	Sharpe ratio	0.937	0.763	0.625	0.541		
Market-cap weighting (2/1991–8/2017	Geometric mean (%)	9.46	9.26	10.32	8.40	Mixed	Mixed
	Arithmetic mean (%)	10.16	10.37	12.21	12.69		
	Standard dev. (%)	11.26	14.24	18.42	27.73		
	Sharpe ratio	0.656	0.534	0.51	0.356		

Table 6.14. **Correlation Analysis**

	Brand Q4 – Q1	Moat No – Wide	Reputation Q4 – Q1	Coskewness Q4 – Q1	Lottery Q4 – Q1	SMB (size)	HML (value)
A. Equal-weighted composites							
Brand	100%	14%	16%	10%	−14%	25%	6%
Moat	14	100	44	0	−86	63	28
Reputation	16	44	100	19	−41	38	54
Coskewness	10	0	19	100	−1	7	29
Lottery	−14	−86	−41	−1	100	−64	−23
SMB	25	63	38	7	−64	100	30
HML	6	28	54	29	−23	30	100
B. Market cap–weighted composites							
Brand	100%	7%	51%	18%	14%	4%	9%
Moat	7	100	33	−2	−75	62	27
Reputation	51	33	100	18	−12	22	47
Coskewness	18	−2	18	100	4	17	17
Lottery	14	−75	−12	4	100	−53	−17
SMB	4	62	22	17	−53	100	30
HML	9	27	47	17	−17	30	100

A reasonable question to ask is how these various potential dimensions of popularity relate to the Fama–French SMB and HML factors, which we obtained from the French Data Library.[45] To approach an answer, for each of the analyses in this chapter, we created a "factor" series by subtracting the monthly return of the popular quartile portfolio from that of the unpopular quartile portfolio, where applicable. (For the moat factor, we subtracted the returns of the wide-moat portfolio from those of the no-moat portfolio.) Then, based on the maximum common time period, July 2002 through August 2017, we calculated the correlation matrix of the five characteristics that we studied plus SMB and HML. Panel A of **Table 6.14** displays the equally weighted results, and Panel B displays the market cap–weighted results.

We found the correlations between the various factors to be relatively low. Moving across the measures of brand value, competitive advantage, and reputation, representing three dimensions of popularity, we see that the

---

[45]http://mba.tuck.dartmouth.edu/pages/faculty/ken.french/data_library.html.

arithmetic and geometric mean returns of the less popular quartiles nearly monotonically outperformed the more popular quartiles. The higher returns for the quartiles based on brand power had no discernible relationship to risk. The higher returns based on sustainable competitive advantage had a strong relationship to risk (more risk/more return), and those based on company reputation had a mild relationship to risk.

Assuming that a powerful brand, a sustainable competitive advantage, and a good reputation are characteristics that investors like or admire, from the popularity perspective, some investors (the willing or unknowing losers) are simply willing to give up some level of return or overpay for a characteristic they like.

The results based on sustainable competitive advantage and company reputation are consistent with the risk–return paradigm, but the results from all three data sets are consistent with the theory of popularity.

We performed empirical analyses for negatively coskewed stocks and lottery-like stocks. Stocks with negative coskewness were expected to command a higher expected return than those with positive coskewness because negatively skewed returns are less desirable or less popular. Lottery-like stocks have a relatively small probability of a large payoff and are preferred. Consistent with the popularity hypothesis, we found that stocks with more negative coskewness (those less popular) tend to have higher risk-adjusted returns and lottery-type stocks (those more popular) tend to have lower risk-adjusted returns.

Overall, we carried out five extended analyses (brand, competitive advantage, reputation, tail risk, and lottery-like stocks). For each, we analyzed both equally weighted composites and market cap–weighted composites. Of the 10 views, 10 out of 10 were highly consistent to moderately consistent with the popularity thesis, whereas only 5 out of 10 were consistent with the risk–return paradigm.

Finally, for each dimension of popularity analyzed in the chapter, we created what one might label "a popularity factor series" by subtracting the most popular portfolio from the least popular portfolio, resulting in a zero-dollar factor for investment brand, competitive advantage, reputation, tail risk, and lottery-like stocks. We carried out this approach for both the equally weighted composites and the market cap–weighted composites. We created correlation matrixes so we could see how correlated the various factors were with one another and with the Fama–French size and value factors. We found the correlations between the various factors to be relatively low.

7. Empirical Evidence of Popularity from Factors

Throughout this book, we have touched on the idea that popularity helps to explain most, if not all, of the well-known premiums and anomalies. We have even been able to put forth popularity as a potential explanation for the equity premium puzzle, the underdiversification puzzle, momentum, and bubbles and crashes. In this chapter, we take a closer look at various return premiums and anomalies through the popularity lens.

This chapter is largely based on Ibbotson and Kim (2017; hereafter, IK) with an overlay of the popularity framework of Ibbotson and Idzorek (2014) and Idzorek and Ibbotson (2017), which has been advanced throughout this book. Specifically, IK studied the risk and return relationships that are revealed when stocks are sorted by beta, volatility, size, value, liquidity, and momentum. All of the tables and figures in this chapter are based on the tables and figures in IK, with some recasting, reordering, and reformatting.

As the reader will see, the conventional wisdom that more risk means more return does not always hold. We believe that popularity serves as a good explanation for this.

Returns and Factors

IK used the CRSP data set (market data) and Compustat data set (accounting data) for US stocks as accessed through the WRDS website.[46] They constructed portfolios annually on the final trading day of each calendar year between 1971 and 2016 and used trailing 12-month ("selection year") data. For each year, the universe was limited to a maximum of 3,000 stocks, but in about half of the sample period years, the universe consisted of fewer than 3,000 stocks after the sample was culled for small-capitalization stocks, low stock prices, or missing data.[47] We made use of selection-year data on

---

[46]The WRDS (Wharton Research Data Services) website is at wrds-web.wharton.upenn. edu. CRSP (Center for Research in Security Prices) data are from the University of Chicago, Booth School of Business. The Compustat data are from Standard & Poor's, which is a division of the McGraw-Hill Companies.

[47]The inclusion criteria for stocks were as follows: common stocks listed on the New York Stock Exchange, the American Stock Exchange and successor exchanges, or the NASDAQ exchange but excluding real estate investment trusts, warrants, American depositary receipts, exchange-traded funds, Americus Trust components, and closed-end funds. Data for trading volume, total returns, earnings, shares outstanding, and price had to be available for the 12 months of the selection year. The stock price at the end of the selection year had to be at least $2.

Table 7.1. Composite Returns for the Universe, 1972–2016

Weighting	Statistics	
Equally weighted	Geometric mean return	12.52%
	Arithmetic mean return	14.66
	Standard deviation	21.56
Cap-weighted	Geometric mean return	10.56
	Arithmetic mean return	12.02
	Standard deviation	17.34

Source: Ibbotson and Kim (2017).

revenue, earnings, book equity, and assets when available. Selected portfolios were passively held for the following calendar year (the "performance year") to determine the total returns of the portfolios.

Table 7.1 presents summary statistics for the equally weighted and cap-weighted composites derived from the universe of stocks in the IK study. The period consists of 45 performance years from 1972 to 2016 (1971 was used only as a selection year), during which the average number of stocks in the universe portfolio was 2,603. This period covered several economic cycles, including the recessions of 1973–1974, 1980–1981, 1991–1992, and 2000–2001 as well as the financial crisis of 2008. It also includes the strong bull markets of the 1980s, 1990s, and 2009–2016, so the overall returns are still reasonably high and are far in excess of riskless rates. Relative to the returns on cash and bonds (not reported), a substantial equity risk premium was realized over the period regardless of the weighting scheme. As Table 7.1 shows, the equally weighted composite produced a higher geometric return, albeit with a higher standard deviation, than the cap-weighted composite and is thus consistent with the risk–return paradigm.

IK examined beta, volatility, size, value, liquidity, momentum, and other factors based on these variables. From this list, we examined those variables that are most relevant to empirical tests of popularity.[48] From our perspective, among active managers, high beta, high volatility, and high liquidity are popular characteristics. High volatility is popular among active managers because of the commonly held belief that a portfolio of high-beta stocks should

---

Finally, the market cap of included companies had to rank within the largest 3,000 for the year and exceed a fixed fraction of the aggregate market cap at year end, equal to that of a $140 million company at the end of 2014.

[48]In particular, we did not include Fama–French regression coefficients because they may not be indicative of underlying characteristics, such as size or value.

outperform a portfolio of low-beta stocks in most markets since the stock market goes up most years. Portfolio managers know that most investors focus primarily on returns and return comparisons and often ignore risk-adjusted returns or treat them as less important than pure returns. Of the IK factors, we viewed momentum as a change or a series of changes in relative popularity.

For each factor, IK sorted all stocks in the universe in the selection year and formed quartiles. They then measured the total returns of the quartile portfolios in the following performance year.

IK numbered the quartiles on the basis of *ex post* performance over the 45-year period, so Quartile 1 outperformed Quartile 4. For consistency with Chapter 6, we renumbered IK's quartiles, where possible, on the basis of popularity so that Quartile 1 contains the most popular stocks and Quartile 4 contains the least popular stocks.

Table 7.2 presents the median factor values for the various quartile portfolios constructed on the last trading day of selection year 2015. For example, the row labeled "Beta" lists the median beta of the four quartile portfolios constructed by sorting each stock in the universe by beta (as calculated from

Table 7.2. Median "Factor" Metric of All Quartile Portfolios Selected in 2015

Factor(s)	Portfolio Sorting Metric	Q4 (least popular)	Q3	Q2	Q1 (most popular)
Beta & volatility	Beta	0.667	0.885	1.042	1.310
	Daily volatility	0.013	0.017	0.023	0.036
	Monthly volatility	0.051	0.072	0.101	0.162
Size	Market cap ($ billions)	0.259	0.792	2.273	11.577
	Total assets ($ billions)	0.240	1.017	3.229	15.735
	Revenue ($ billions)	0.099	0.529	1.793	8.211
	Net income ($ billions)	−0.042	0.019	0.094	0.559
Value	Book/market	0.983	0.559	0.315	0.126
	Earnings/price	0.084	0.053	0.028	−0.066
	Return on equity	−0.223	0.057	0.115	0.250
Liquidity	Amihud illiquidity	2.948	0.432	0.085	0.013
Momentum	12-month	−0.373	−0.114	0.064	0.319
	2–12 months	−0.319	−0.070	0.101	0.358

Note: Amihud illiquidity is the Amihud (2002) measure, defined as the absolute value of the daily return divided by the daily dollar value of shares traded, averaged over the course of a period.
Source: Ibbotson and Kim (2017).

daily stock returns during 2015). Similarly, the row labeled "Market cap" shows the median market cap (in billions of dollars) of the four size quartiles constructed using year-end 2015 market-cap data. In some rows, we have reversed the order of the values shown by IK to conform to our convention for numbering the quartiles.

IK lagged accounting data two months beyond the end of the accounting reporting period to reflect reporting delays. Thus, in Table 7.2, the metrics of total assets, revenue, net income, book/market, earnings/price, and return on equity for selection year 2015 were based on accounting data from reporting periods ending between November 2014 and October 2015. In contrast, we used calendar year 2015 data to rank market cap and momentum because these variables are immediately available at the end of the year.

IK constructed portfolios on the last day of the selection year (1971–2015) and then measured performance in the subsequent year (1972–2016). During the performance year, they did not rebalance, so the position weights floated throughout the performance year. Therefore, the end of each calendar year marked both the end of the performance year for the portfolios selected one year previously and the construction date for a new set of selection-year portfolios based on the recalculated sorting metrics listed in Table 7.2. All of the quartile portfolios listed were rebalanced annually.

We report the annualized geometric mean, the annualized arithmetic mean, and the annualized monthly standard deviation in the tables that follow. In the figures that follow, we show the annualized geometric mean during the study period plotted on the vertical axes and the annualized standard deviations plotted on the horizontal axes. In the sections that follow, we focus on beta and volatility, size, value, and liquidity.

Beta and Volatility

According to the capital asset pricing model (CAPM), a positive relationship should exist between beta and returns. In general, a positive relationship should exist between risk and return. Thus, higher volatility and systematic risk should also be associated with higher returns.

Table 7.3 reports the long-term performance-year returns for each quartile portfolio based on beta and also based on volatility. For the reasons that we discussed in Chapter 2, we regard high-beta and high-volatility stocks as being popular and low-beta and low-volatility stocks as being unpopular.

IK showed the annualized geometric mean, arithmetic mean, and annualized standard deviation that were realized during the study period. For all but one sorting metric (daily volatility), Quartile 4 (Q4) outperformed the other quartiles, in terms of geometric mean return, over the study period.

Table 7.3. Beta and Volatility Quartile Portfolio Returns, 1972–2016

Portfolio Sorting Metric	Statistic	Q4 (least popular, low)	Q3	Q2	Q1 (most popular, high)
CAPM beta	Geometric mean return (%)	14.20	13.99	12.45	8.24
	Arithmetic mean return (%)	15.70	15.92	14.82	12.20
	Standard dev. (%)	18.15	20.67	22.72	29.24
	Sharpe ratio	0.60	0.53	0.44	0.25
Daily volatility	Geometric mean return (%)	13.94	14.18	13.24	7.12
	Arithmetic mean return (%)	15.15	15.91	15.78	11.81
	Standard dev. (%)	16.25	19.47	23.51	32.21
	Sharpe ratio	0.63	0.57	0.46	0.22
Monthly volatility	Geometric mean return (%)	14.28	14.27	12.78	7.35
	Arithmetic mean return (%)	15.56	16.07	15.35	11.67
	Standard dev. (%)	16.93	19.84	23.57	30.90
	Sharpe ratio	0.63	0.56	0.44	0.22

Source: Ibbotson and Kim (2017).

In each case, Q4 represents the most unpopular stocks (low beta, low daily volatility, and low monthly volatility) from the selection year.

In Table 7.3, the less popular quartiles monotonically outperformed the more popular quartiles from a Sharpe ratio perspective. The same is nearly true from a geometric return perspective. The quartiles based on CAPM beta, daily volatility, and monthly volatility are all consistent with the popularity paradigm, while none of them is consistent with the risk–return paradigm. In fact, the breakdown of the risk–return relationship in Table 7.3 is dramatic.

Figure 7.1 plots the annual geometric mean versus the annualized standard deviation of the quartile portfolios in Table 7.3. The equally weighted stock universe reported in Figure 7.1 and in the rest of the figures in this chapter is labeled "Universe Equal," and the cap-weighted stock universe is labeled "Universe Cap."

By a relatively large margin, Figure 7.1 shows that the three Q1 portfolios (high CAPM beta, high monthly volatility, and high daily volatility) have the lowest realized returns and highest standard deviations. The Q3 and Q4 portfolios have the highest returns and lower standard deviations.

Other researchers have found similar results in which the expected relationship—more risk/more return—seems to break down. For example, Jensen, Black, and Scholes (1972) and Frazzini and Pedersen (2014) found

Figure 7.1. Performance of Beta and Volatility Quartile Portfolios, 1972–2016

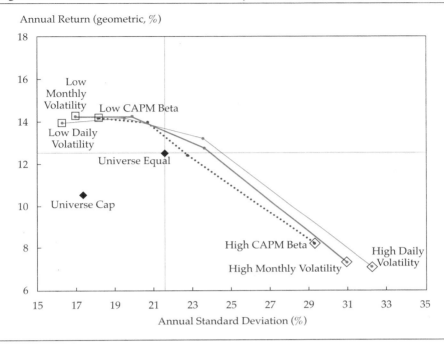

Notes: Squares indicate Q4 (least popular, low), and diamonds indicate Q1 (most popular, high). Small dots indicate Q2 and Q3.
Source: Ibbotson and Kim (2017).

that high-beta stocks are associated with low excess returns; Haugen and Baker (1991) and Ang, Hodrick, Xing, and Zhang (2006) found that high-volatility stocks consistently underperform.

As we discussed in Chapter 2, building on the idea of leverage aversion put forth by Black (1972), Frazzini and Pedersen (2014) argued that leverage aversion on the part of enough market participants results in demand for high-volatility, high-beta securities.[49] The reason is that investors who cannot or do not wish to leverage may buy high-beta securities as a substitute. The popularity of high-beta stocks, in turn, bids up prices and reduces returns. To the extent to which leverage is highly unpopular and investors are averse to it, Frazzini and Pedersen's results are consistent with the theory of popularity.

The results that we present in Figure 7.1 show that the CAPM risk–return relationship does not hold. Although risk is usually unpopular, especially

---

[49]See Note 21 in Chapter 2.

across asset classes, in some situations, taking risk is the popular thing to do, especially in the stock market. Thus, we see that beta and volatility have had an inverse empirical relationship to stock returns, with high-beta and high-volatility stocks having lower returns.

Size

Table 7.4 presents results for the size quartile portfolios. Because the geometric return of the Q4 (small-cap, least popular) portfolio is higher than that of the Q1 (large-cap, most popular) portfolio, we conclude that the small-cap premium is positive. Additionally, small-cap stocks have a higher standard deviation than large-cap stocks; thus, the size dimension as measured by market cap is consistent with a positive risk–return trade-off. If we interpret market cap as a relative dollar-based popularity vote, this result is perhaps an indirect measurement of popularity. Relative to small-cap stocks, more people own large-cap stocks and own more of them, and large-cap stocks

Table 7.4. Performance of Size Quartile Portfolio Returns, 1972–2016

Portfolio Sorting Metric	Statistic	Q4 (least popular, smallest)	Q3	Q2	Q1 (most popular, largest)
Market cap	Geometric mean return (%)	13.27	12.32	12.45	11.48
	Arithmetic mean return (%)	16.43	14.74	14.45	13.01
	Standard dev. (%)	26.50	23.15	20.89	17.83
	Sharpe ratio	0.44	0.43	0.46	0.46
Total assets	Geometric mean return (%)	10.48	12.72	13.90	12.60
	Arithmetic mean return (%)	13.84	14.98	15.69	14.30
	Standard dev. (%)	27.27	22.14	19.84	18.92
	Sharpe ratio	0.33	0.46	0.55	0.50
Revenue	Geometric mean return (%)	10.20	13.07	13.19	13.42
	Arithmetic mean return (%)	13.25	15.36	15.23	15.11
	Standard dev. (%)	26.07	22.37	21.07	19.06
	Sharpe ratio	0.32	0.47	0.49	0.54
Net income	Geometric mean return (%)	9.92	13.64	13.28	12.57
	Arithmetic mean return (%)	13.79	16.00	15.05	14.04
	Standard dev. (%)	29.19	22.67	19.73	17.69
	Sharpe ratio	0.31	0.49	0.52	0.52

Source: Ibbotson and Kim (2017).

are more liquid, are better known, and are covered by more equity analysts. Hence, large-cap stocks have a number of popular characteristics.

In addition to market cap, Table 7.4 presents statistics on quartile portfolios based on three alternative measures of company size: total assets, revenue, and net income. When these measures are used, the largest companies outperform the smallest. This result is consistent with previous empirical research, such as that of Berk (1997), who explored the relationship between accounting-based measures of company size and returns, although Berk did not attribute the cause of this result to popularity as we do.

Regardless of the metric used, the standard deviation of returns is much higher for the small companies than for the large companies. As Table 7.4 shows, high volatility is associated with small size, however defined. For *small-cap companies*, high risk is associated with high returns, whereas for *companies that were small based on other metrics*, high risk is associated with low returns. **Figure 7.2** shows this graphically.

Why do small-cap companies tend to outperform when larger companies measured by total assets, revenue, and total net income outperform? We believe small-cap companies are unpopular because they are riskier, less liquid, and so on, but we also believe that larger companies based on high assets, high revenue, or high net income can be relatively unpopular or overlooked on a relative basis.

Most importantly, we believe that the popularity effect is most pronounced when investors seem to nearly uniformly agree about whether an attribute or characteristic is desirable or undesirable. Market cap seems to be something that matters to most investors, to the degree that it can drive decision making; or to put it differently, perhaps it is a direct barometer of the aggregate decisions made by investors. In contrast, few investors make decisions exclusively on the basis of such metrics as assets, revenue, or total net income, and to interpret these factors as a reflection of investor preference would be challenging. When it comes to decision making, these metrics are almost always combined with some other data point(s) to arrive at a metric that influences decision making.

Value

The value effect is one of the best known violations of the CAPM, being first documented by Basu (1977). (See also Stattman 1980 and Basu 1983). Value tends to outperform growth over long periods for various measures of value. The results in **Table 7.5** confirm these results for our quartile portfolios formed by ranking stocks based on book/market (B/M) and earnings/price

Figure 7.2. Risk and Return of Size Quartile Portfolios, 1972–2016

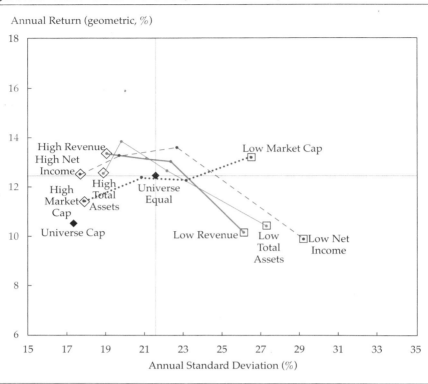

Annual Return (geometric, %)

Note: Squares indicate Q4 (smallest), and diamonds indicate Q1 (largest). Small dots indicate Q2 and Q3.
Source: Ibbotson and Kim (2017).

(E/P).[50] In each case, the Quartile 4 (least popular) portfolio outperformed the Quartile 1 (most popular) portfolio.

Figure 7.3 plots the geometric mean return and standard deviation of return for the four value quartile portfolios for the two measures of value. Note that, although the Q4 value (least popular) portfolio clearly outperforms in each case, the Q1 growth (most popular) portfolio is usually the riskiest, even though it has the lowest returns. Thus, value premiums appear to be

---

[50]IK included return on equity (ROE) as a measure of value. Because ROE is based on book value, however, rather than market value (as is the case with both B/M and E/P), we do not regard it as a measure of value. Furthermore, because the market cap or share price of a stock is the denominator in B/M and E/P and market cap is an indirect indicator of popularity, B/M and E/P are clearly related to popularity.

Table 7.5. Value Quartile Portfolio Returns, 1972–2016

Portfolio Sorting Metric	Statistic	Q4 (least popular, high)	Q3	Q2	Q1 (most popular, low)
B/M	Geometric mean return (%)	15.77	13.91	11.48	8.23
	Arithmetic mean return (%)	18.43	15.85	13.47	11.00
	Standard dev. (%)	24.50	20.98	20.55	24.32
	Sharpe ratio	0.55	0.52	0.42	0.25
E/P	Geometric mean return (%)	16.10	13.86	10.89	8.22
	Arithmetic mean return (%)	18.42	15.55	12.85	11.83
	Standard dev. (%)	22.77	19.52	20.33	27.93
	Sharpe ratio	0.60	0.55	0.39	0.25

Source: Ibbotson and Kim (2017).

Figure 7.3. Risk and Return of Value Quartile Portfolios, 1972–2016

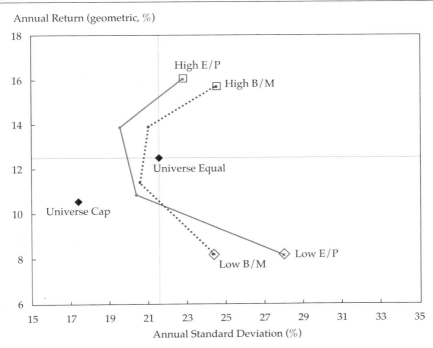

Notes: Squares indicate Q4 (least popular, high), and diamonds indicate Q1 (most popular, low). Small dots indicate Q2 and Q3.
Source: Ibbotson and Kim (2017).

positive but are not necessarily risk premiums, as they are sometimes referred to (see Fama and French 1992).

High-growth companies, whether characterized by low B/M or low E/P, tend to be the newsworthy, up-and-coming, "hot" companies. But again, the most popular stocks have the worst performance.

Liquidity

To measure liquidity, IK used the Amihud (2002) illiquidity metric, defined as the absolute value of the daily return divided by the daily dollar value of shares traded, averaged over the course of the selection year. IK ranked stocks during the selection year with this metric and placed them into the four quartile portfolios for each performance year.

Table 7.6 shows the returns for the illiquidity quartile portfolios. Q4 is the low-liquidity (highest illiquidity, least popular) portfolio and Q1 is the high-liquidity (lowest illiquidity, most popular) portfolio. Q4 outperformed Q1 by a wide margin. This result makes sense because liquidity is always desired by some segments of the market, and those investors are willing to pay for it.

Momentum

Table 7.7 presents results for the returns of quartile portfolios formed from ranking the returns on the last 12 months and on the last 11 months (2–12) as of calendar year-end. The 11-month measure is often used because the near-in month is usually considered a reversal month (Jegadeesh 1990). The results show that when either measure is used, a momentum effect occurred in the period.

Figure 7.4 shows the geometric mean return plotted against standard deviation of returns for the quartile portfolios formed on the two measures of momentum. As shown, the low-momentum portfolio (Q4) not only has the worst performance, but it also has the highest risk. As far as our analysis

Table 7.6. Illiquidity Quartile Portfolio Returns, 1972–2016

Portfolio Sorting Metric	Statistic	Q4 (least popular, least liquid)	Q3	Q2	Q1 (most popular, most liquid)
Amihud illiquidity	Geometric mean return (%)	14.48	11.95	11.97	11.22
	Arithmetic mean return (%)	17.16	14.46	14.16	12.87
	Standard dev. (%)	24.55	23.50	21.83	18.53
	Sharpe ratio	0.50	0.41	0.43	0.43

Source: Ibbotson and Kim (2017).

Table 7.7. Momentum Quartile Portfolio Returns, 1972–2016

Portfolio Sorting Metric	Statistic	Q4 (low)	Q3	Q2	Q1 (high)
12-month momentum	Geometric mean return (%)	8.20	13.40	14.38	13.07
	Arithmetic mean return (%)	11.90	15.27	16.03	15.45
	Standard dev. (%)	28.61	20.38	19.11	22.87
	Sharpe ratio	0.25	0.51	0.58	0.46
2–12 month momentum	Geometric mean return (%)	8.39	13.05	14.46	13.25
	Arithmetic mean return (%)	11.98	14.86	16.23	15.58
	Standard dev. (%)	28.17	19.97	19.75	22.65
	Sharpe ratio	0.25	0.50	0.58	0.47

Source: Ibbotson and Kim (2017).

Figure 7.4. Risk and Return of Momentum Quartile Portfolios, 1972–2016

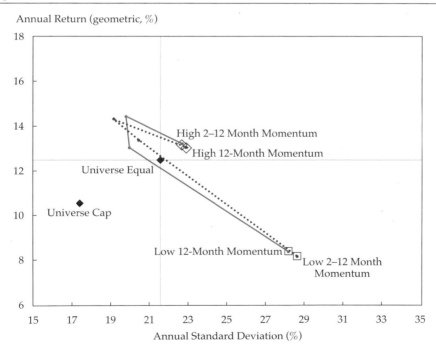

Notes: Squares indicate Q4 (low), and diamonds indicate Q1 (high). Small dots indicate Q2 and Q3.
Source: Ibbotson and Kim (2017).

goes, momentum is a special case. Although it fits well with the popularity framework, it does not fit well with our cross-sectional testing method. We view high-momentum stocks as stocks that are *increasing in popularity*—that is, becoming higher priced. But why do high-momentum stocks in one year continue to outperform the next year? Empirically, the increase in popularity is sustained over a relatively long period of time, such as 6–18 months. Ultimately, we believe that these stocks become overly popular, resulting in a reversal, but the reversal is not immediate and appears to be a market inefficiency. Stocks do not appear to immediately react to new information; their price changes continue over long periods in the same general direction.

Table 7.8 consolidates the previous analyses and presents our assessment of how the results are or are not consistent with the popularity framework and/or the more-risk/more-return paradigm. We found that 7 out of 10 of the

Table 7.8. Summary Results for Factor Portfolios and Consistency with Asset Pricing Frameworks, 1972–2016

Characteristic	Statistic	Least Popular Q4	Q3	Q2	Most Popular Q1	Consistent with Popularity	Consistent with More Risk/More Return
CAPM Beta	Geometric	14.20	13.99	12.45	8.24	Yes	No
	Arithmetic	15.70	15.92	14.82	12.20		
	Std. dev.	18.15	20.67	22.72	29.24		
	Sharpe ratio return (%)	0.6	0.53	0.44	0.25		
Daily Volatility	Geometric	13.94	14.18	13.24	7.12	Yes	No
	Arithmetic	15.15	15.91	15.78	11.81		
	Std. dev.	16.25	19.47	23.51	32.21		
	Sharpe ratio	0.63	0.57	0.46	0.22		
Monthly Volatility	Geometric	14.28	14.27	12.78	7.35	Yes	No
	Arithmetic	15.56	16.07	15.35	11.67		
	Std. dev.	16.93	19.84	23.57	30.90		
	Sharpe ratio	0.63	0.56	0.44	0.22		
Market Cap	Geometric	13.27	12.32	12.45	11.48	Yes	Yes
	Arithmetic	16.43	14.74	14.45	13.01		
	Std. dev.	26.50	23.15	20.89	17.83		
	Sharpe ratio	0.44	0.43	0.46	0.46		

(continued)

Table 7.8. Summary Results for Factor Portfolios and Consistency with Asset Pricing Frameworks, 1972–2016 (continued)

Characteristic	Statistic	Least Popular Q4	Q3	Q2	Most Popular Q1	Consistent with Popularity	Consistent with More Risk/More Return
Total Assets	Geometric	10.48	12.72	13.90	12.60	No	No
	Arithmetic	13.84	14.98	15.69	14.30		
	Std. dev.	27.27	22.14	19.84	18.92		
	Sharpe ratio	0.33	0.46	0.55	0.5		
Revenue	Geometric	10.20	13.07	13.19	13.42	No	No
	Arithmetic	13.25	15.36	15.23	15.11		
	Std. dev.	26.07	22.37	21.07	19.06		
	Sharpe ratio	0.32	0.47	0.49	0.54		
Net Income	Geometric	9.92	13.64	13.28	12.57	No	No
	Arithmetic	13.79	16.00	15.05	14.04		
	Std. dev.	29.19	22.67	19.73	17.69		
	Sharpe ratio	0.31	0.49	0.52	0.52		
B/M	Geometric	15.77	13.91	11.48	8.23	Yes	No
	Arithmetic	18.43	15.85	13.47	11.00		
	Std. dev.	24.50	20.98	20.55	24.32		
	Sharpe ratio	0.55	0.52	0.42	0.25		
E/P	Geometric	16.10	13.86	10.89	8.22	Yes	No
	Arithmetic	18.42	15.55	12.85	11.83		
	Std. dev.	22.77	19.52	20.33	27.93		
	Sharpe ratio	0.6	0.55	0.39	0.25		
Amihud Illiquidity	Geometric	14.48	11.95	11.97	11.22	Yes	Yes
	Arithmetic	17.16	14.46	14.16	12.87		
	Std. dev.	24.55	23.50	21.83	18.53		
	Sharpe ratio	0.5	0.41	0.43	0.43		

Notes: All quartile portfolios are equally weighted. "Geometric" and "Arithmetic" refer to mean returns and are given in percentages; "Std. dev." is standard deviation and is given in percentage.

analyses are consistent with the popularity framework, whereas only 2 out of 10 are consistent with the more-risk/more-return paradigm.

We deem three measured characteristics to be inconsistent with the popularity framework—high total assets, high revenue, and high net income. Although these three are characteristics that investors should like (thus making them popular), we believe they are almost never viewed in isolation and they are almost never the sole reason that an investment decision is made. Therefore, we do not interpret these results as definitive evidence against the popularity framework.

Conclusion

In this chapter, we analyzed the applicable quartile portfolios from IK through the popularity lens. IK ranked stocks and formed quartile portfolios on the basis of beta, volatility, size of companies, value measures, liquidity, and momentum, which we interpreted to be indicators of or characteristics associated with popularity. Rankings were all done in a selection year, and the ranked quartile portfolio returns were measured in the following (out of sample) performance year for the period 1972–2016.

Classical finance tells us that, in general, greater reward comes with greater systematic risk. IK found, however, that low-beta and low-volatility portfolios outperform high-beta and high-volatility portfolios. Also, small-cap stocks outperform but not small companies; large companies, as measured by assets, revenue, and income, outperform. The less liquid stocks outperform with more risk. High-momentum portfolios outperform, as anticipated, but the low-momentum portfolios are riskier.

Overall, the characteristics of the best performing portfolios are high E/P and high B/M. On a risk-adjusted basis, the best performers are low-beta and low-volatility portfolios.

When considered individually, the results presented here mainly confirm previously reported results. By presenting these results together in a common framework, however, we have shown a clear negative relationship between risk and return in the US stock market during the period studied. A common theme has emerged. Although risk is often unpopular, it can be popular in certain circumstances; often, characteristics other than risk dominate returns in the stock market.

Of the 10 factors analyzed in this chapter, we found that 7 are consistent with the popularity framework but only 2 of 10 are consistent with the classical view that more risk means more return. For the three factors that were not consistent with the popularity framework—larger companies based on high assets, high revenue, or high net income—we believe these are attributes that are almost always coupled with market capitalization to form valuation ratios. As standalone measures, investors do not uniformly agree about whether these characteristics are desirable or undesirable.

8. Summary and Conclusions

To summarize the concepts and findings that we have presented in this book, we classify them into popularity as a concept, popularity as a bridge between theories, popularity as a theory, and empirical evidence for popularity.

Popularity as a Concept

Popularity is how much anything is liked, preferred, or desired. We applied the concept to assets and securities. In this way, we were able to give explanations for all the premiums in the markets, especially the stock market.

- Most assets and securities are in relatively fixed supply over the short or intermediate term. Popularity represents the demand or perhaps the excess demand for a security and is thus an important determinant of prices for a set of expected cash flows.

- The "risk" premiums in the market are payoffs for the *riskiness* of securities. In classical finance, investors are risk averse and market frictions are usually assumed away. Risk is unpopular. The largest risk premium is the equity risk premium—that is, the extra expected return for investing in equities rather than bonds or risk-free assets. Other risk premiums include the interest rate risk and default risk in bond markets.

- The market encompasses many premiums that may or may not be related to risk, but all are related to investing in something that is unpopular in some way. We analyzed premiums on security characteristics that are systematically unpopular, although they can change dynamically over time. Such premiums include the following:

  - the size premium,
  - the value premium,
  - the liquidity premium,
  - the premium for severe downside risk,
  - low-volatility and low-beta premiums,
  - premiums and discounts for environmental, social, and governance investing,

- premiums for lack of competitive advantage, poor brand awareness, and poor reputation, and

- the premium for any type of security that is being overlooked.

- Assets and securities that are only temporarily popular or unpopular are considered to be mispriced. We did not focus on mispricing in this book.

Popularity as a Bridge between Classical and Behavioral Finance

The title of this book refers to popularity as a bridge between classical and behavioral finance. Both approaches to finance rest on investor preferences, which we recast as popularity.

- Classical finance is based on the following principles: rationality, equilibrium or risk-free arbitrage, and efficient markets with "fair" pricing. In this book, we took the equilibrium approach.

- In classical finance, risk—in particular, systematic risk—is the primary aversion of investors. A single systematic risk is priced in the capital asset pricing model (CAPM), but some risks, including various types of stock or bond risks, can also be multidimensional. The specific structure of risk can also be priced, as in catastrophic risk.

- Although classical finance usually assumes away market frictions, rational investors may have preferences for market liquidity, favorable tax treatments, or asset divisibility, making assets more or less valuable to the extent they embody these characteristics.

- In behavioral finance, investors may not be completely rational. Thus, investors may have preferences that go beyond rational behavior.

- We classified behavioral biases into two types, psychological and cognitive. Psychological desires cause some assets to be more popular than others, relative to their risk-adjusted expected cash flows and relative to such other rational characteristics as liquidity. Investors' rationality is also limited because they make cognitive errors.

- Neoclassical economics provides the rationality framework for efficient capital markets, CAPM, New Equilibrium Theory (NET), and so on. Behavioral economics assumes limited or "bounded" rationality and thus provides the framework for prospect theory, loss aversion, framing, mental accounting, overconfidence, and similar cognitive biases.

- Popularity represents preferences, which can be rational or irrational. Thus, popularity provides a bridge between classical and behavioral finance.

Popularity as a Theory

The CAPM is an elegant and easy-to-use theory for describing investor expected returns in an equilibrium setting. We generalized the CAPM to include all types of preferences in the popularity asset pricing model (PAPM).

- The CAPM assumes that investors are not only rational and risk averse but can also diversify away all unsystematic risk. Thus, only systematic (market) risk in securities is priced. Securities with high systematic risk have lower relative prices and, therefore, higher expected returns.

- NET is a framework in which investors are rational but have preferences for or aversions to various security characteristics beyond undiversifiable market risk, as in the CAPM—even beyond the multiple dimensions of risk modeled in the arbitrage pricing theory.

- In NET, in addition to systematic risk aversion, investors also have a rational aversion to assets that are difficult to diversify, lack liquidity, are highly taxed, and/or are not easily divisible. All these preferences affect the prices and expected returns of assets that embody these characteristics.

- The PAPM provides a theory in a CAPM equilibrium framework by including both risk aversion and popularity preferences on the part of investors. These preferences can be rational, as in NET, or irrational, as in behavioral economics.

- In the PAPM, the various securities have different systematic and unsystematic risks and differing popularity characteristics. Investors also have differing risk aversions and popularity preferences. The characteristics are priced according to the *aggregate* demand for each of the characteristics. The expected return of each security is determined by its risk and popularity characteristics.

- In our PAPM illustration, one investor, having only risk aversion and no popularity preferences, was purely rational. Although this investor earned excess economic returns, he or she was only part of the equilibrium demand, so aggregate popularity was still a part of PAPM pricing. Securities are priced in this equilibrium framework, and no riskless arbitrage opportunities exist.

Empirical Evidence for Popularity

The concept of a negative return to popularity (what we have simply called "popularity") has been shown to be consistent with the empirical premiums found in the stock market. But this explanation is after the fact. Direct tests involve trying to identify in advance what characteristics are likely to be popular and which ones are likely to be unpopular and then to test the relative performance of portfolios based on them. We did this test at the company level and at the common stock level.

- We carried out analyses on five characteristics: (1) brand, (2) competitive advantage, (3) reputation, (4) tail risk, and (5) lottery-like stocks. In the analyses, we considered both equally weighted composites and market cap–weighted composites. Of these 10 different views, all 10 are highly consistent to moderately consistent with popularity whereas only 5 of 10 are consistent with the paradigm that more risk equals more return.

- Companies with high brand values are popular. The quartile portfolios containing these companies ended up having significantly lower returns than the quartile portfolios with the lowest brand value over the April 2000–August 2017 period.

- Companies with sustainable competitive advantages are said to have wide economic moats, making them more popular than low-moat or no-moat companies. Portfolios of companies with no moats outperformed portfolios of wide-moat companies over the July 2002–August 2017 period.

- Quartile portfolios of companies with better reputations tended to underperform quartile portfolios of companies with less glowing reputations over the April 2000–August 2017 period.

- Equities that have historically had negative tail-risk events (low or negative coskewness) are unpopular. Quartile portfolios of these stocks significantly outperformed those of stocks with high coskewness over the January 1996–August 2017 period.

- Stocks with lottery-like payoffs are popular because they provide the apparent opportunity for outsized gains. Quartile portfolios of these stocks, specifically those with the highest average of their five best days' returns, had the lowest risk-adjusted returns among the quartile portfolios based on this measure of lottery-like payoffs over the February 1991–December 2016 period.

- We also examined the well-known premiums and anomalies for the 1972–2016 period by analyzing 10 applicable sets of factor-based quartile portfolios in Ibbotson and Kim (2017) through the popularity lens. Ibbotson and Kim found that quartile portfolios of low-beta, low-volatility, small-capitalization, value, less liquidity, and high-momentum stocks outperformed their opposites. Of the 10 factors that we analyzed, 7 are consistent with the popularity framework, whereas only 2 out of 10 are consistent with the classical risk–return view. Overall, we found that for most categories in the stock market, an *inverse* relationship exists between risk and return, counter to classical theory. Either risk is popular in some circumstances or other, nonrisk characteristics dominate returns. We believe that popularity reflects the demand that ultimately determines prices and returns.

Popularity is a framework that can be used to model asset values and expected returns. Most existing financial literature, whether classical or behavioral, is consistent with popularity. Our new research is also consistent with popularity. Thus, popularity is a bridge between classical and behavioral finance.

References

Amihud, Yakov. 2002. "Illiquidity and Stock Returns: Cross-Section and Time-Series Effects." *Journal of Financial Markets* 5 (1): 31–56.

Amihud, Yakov, and Haim Mendelson. 1986. "Asset Pricing and the Bid-Ask Spread." *Journal of Financial Economics* 17 (2): 223–49.

Ang, Andrew. 2014. *Asset Management: A Systematic Approach to Factor Investing*. New York: Oxford University Press.

Ang, Andrew, Robert J. Hodrick, Yuhang Xing, and Xiaoyan Zhang. 2006. "The Cross-Section of Volatility and Expected Returns." *Journal of Finance* 61 (1): 259–99.

Anginer, Deniz, and Meir Statman. 2010. "Stocks of Admired and Spurned Companies." *Journal of Portfolio Management* 36 (3): 71–77.

Arnott, Robert D., Jason Hsu, and Philip Moore. 2005. "Fundamental Indexation." *Financial Analysts Journal* 61 (2): 83–99.

Asness, Clifford S., Andrea Frazzini, and Lasse H. Pedersen. 2012. "Leverage Aversion and Risk Parity." *Financial Analysts Journal* 68 (1): 47–59.

Atukeren, Erdal, and Aylin Seçkin. 2007. "On the Valuation of Psychic Returns to Art Market Investments." *Economic Bulletin* 26 (5): 1–12.

Baker, Malcolm, Brendan Bradley, and Jeffrey Wurgler. 2011. "Benchmarks as Limits to Arbitrage: Understanding the Low-Volatility Anomaly." *Financial Analysts Journal* 67 (1): 40–54.

Baker, Nardin L., and Robert A. Haugen. 2012. "Low Risk Stocks Outperform within All Observable Markets in the World." Available at SSRN.

Bali, Turan, Nusret Cakici, and Robert Whitelaw. 2011. "Maxing Out: Stocks as Lotteries and the Cross-Section of Expected Returns." *Journal of Financial Economics* 99 (2): 427–46.

Bansal, Ravi, and Amir Yaron. 2004. "Risks for the Long Run: A Potential Resolution of Asset Pricing Puzzles." *Journal of Finance* 59 (4): 1481–509.

Banz, Rolf W. 1981. "The Relationship between Return and Market Value of a Common Stock." *Journal of Financial Economics* 9 (1): 3–18.

Barber, Brad M., and Terrance Odean. 2008. "All That Glitters: The Effect of Attention and News on the Buying Behavior of Individual and Institutional Investors." *Review of Financial Studies* 21 (2): 785–818.

Barberis, Nicholas, and Ming Huang. 2008. "Stocks as Lotteries: The Implications of Probability Weighting for Security Prices." *American Economic Review* 98 (5): 2066–100.

Barth, Mary E., Michael Clement, George Foster, and Ron Kasznik. 1998. "Brand Values and Capital Market Valuation." *Review of Accounting Studies* 3 (1–2): 41–68.

Basu, Sanjoy. 1977. "Investment Performance of Common Stocks in Relation to Their Price-Earnings Ratios: A Test of the Efficient Market Hypothesis." *Journal of Finance* 32 (3): 663–82.

————. 1983. "The Relationship between Earnings Yield, Market Value, and Return for NYSE Common Stocks: Further Evidence." *Journal of Financial Economics* 12 (1): 129–56.

Baumol, W.J. 1986. "Unnatural Value: Or Art Investment as Floating Crap Game." *American Economic Review* 76 (2): 10–14.

Benartzi, Shlomo, and Richard Thaler. 1995. "Myopic Loss Aversion and the Equity Premium Puzzle." *Quarterly Journal of Economics* 110 (1): 73–92.

Berk, Jonathan B. 1997. "Does Size Really Matter?" *Financial Analysts Journal* 53 (5): 12–18.

Black, Fischer. 1972. "Capital Market Equilibrium with Restricted Borrowing." *Journal of Business* 45 (3): 444–55.

Black, Fischer, and Myron Scholes. 1973. "The Pricing of Options and Corporate Liabilities." *Journal of Political Economy* 81 (3): 637–54.

Blitz, David, and Pim van Vliet. 2007. "The Volatility Effect: Lower Risk without Lower Return." *Journal of Portfolio Management* 34 (1): 102–13.

Campbell, John Y., and John H. Cochrane. 1999. "By Force of Habit: A Consumption-Based Explanation of Aggregate Supply Market Behavior." *Journal of Political Economy* 107 (2): 205–51.

Candela, Guido, Massimiliano Castellani, and Pierpaolo Pattitoni. 2013. "Reconsidering Psychic Return in Art Investments." *Economics Letters* 118 (2): 351–54.

Carhart, Mark M. 1997. "On Persistence in Mutual Fund Performance." *Journal of Finance* 52 (1): 57–82.

Chanel, Olivier L., Louis-André Gérard-Varet, and Victor Ginsburgh. 1994. "Prices and Returns on Paintings: An Exercise on How to Price the Priceless." *GENEVA PAPERS on Risk and Insurance Theory* 19 (1): 7–21.

Clarke, Roger, Harindra de Silva, and Steven Thorley. 2011. "Minimum Variance Portfolio Composition." *Journal of Portfolio Management* 37 (2): 31–45.

Cochrane, J.H. 2011. "Presidential Address: "Discount Rates." *Journal of Finance* 66 (4): 1047–108.

Constantinides, George. 1983. "Capital Market Equilibrium with Personal Tax." *Econometrica* 51 (3): 611–36.

Cooper, Lisette, Jeremy Evnine, Jeff Finkelman, Kate Huntington, and David Lynch. 2016. "Social Finance and the Postmodern Portfolio: Theory and Practice." *Journal of Wealth Management* 18 (4): 9–21.

Damodaran, Aswath. n.d. "Not Riskless, Not Even Close: Pseudo or Speculative Arbitrage." Slides, Stern School of Business, New York University. http://people.stern.nyu.edu/adamodar/pdfiles/invphilslides/session29.pdf.

Datar, Vinay, Narayan Naik, and Robert Radcliffe. 1998. "Liquidity and Stock Returns: An Alternative Test." *Journal of Financial Markets* 1 (2): 203–19.

Diermeier, Jeffrey J., Roger G. Ibbotson, and Laurence B. Siegel. 1984. "The Supply of Capital Market Returns." *Financial Analysts Journal* 40 (2): 74–80.

Dimson, Elroy, Paul Marsh, and Mike Staunton. 2002. *Triumph of the Optimists: 101 Years of Global Investment Returns*. Princeton, NJ: Princeton University Press.

Duca, John V. 2001. "The Democratization of America's Capital Markets." *Economic and Financial Review*, Dallas Fed (Second Quarter): 10–19.

Fama, Eugene F. 1970. "Efficient Capital Markets: A Review of Theory and Empirical Work." *Journal of Finance* 25 (2): 383–417.

Fama, Eugene F., and Kenneth R. French. 1992. "The Cross-Section of Expected Stock Returns." *Journal of Finance* 47 (2): 427–65.

———. 1993. "Common Risk Factors in the Returns on Stocks and Bonds." *Journal of Financial Economics* 33 (1): 3–56.

———. 1996. "Multifactor Explanations of Asset Pricing Anomalies." *Journal of Finance* 51 (1): 55–84.

Fama, Eugene F., and Richard H. Thaler. 2016. "Are Markets Efficient?" *Chicago Booth Review* (30 June). http://review.chicagobooth.edu/economics/2016/video/are-markets-efficient.

Fehle, Frank, Susan M. Fournier, Thomas J. Madden, and David G. Shrider. 2008. "Brand Value and Asset Pricing." *Quarterly Journal of Finance and Accounting* 47 (1): 3–26.

Fisher, Irving. 1930. *The Theory of Interest*. New York: Macmillan.

Frazzini, Andrea, and Lasse H. Pedersen. 2014. "Betting against Beta." *Journal of Financial Economics* 111 (1): 1–25.

Friedman, Milton. 1953. *Essays in Positive Economics*. Chicago: University of Chicago Press.

Goetzmann, William N., and Roger G. Ibbotson. 2008. "History and the Equity Risk Premium." In *Handbook of the Equity Risk Premium*, edited by R. Mehra, 515–34. North Holland: Elsevier.

Goetzmann, William N., and Alok Kumar. 2008. "Equity Portfolio Diversification." *Review of Finance* 12 (3): 433–63.

Graham, Benjamin. 2006. *The Intelligent Investor*. Revised Edition (originally published in 1949). New York: Harper Collins.

Graham, Benjamin, and David Dodd. 1934. *Security Analysis*. New York: McGraw-Hill.

Green, Jeremiah, John R.M. Hand, and X. Frank Zhang. 2017. "The Characteristics That Provide Independent Information about Average U.S. Monthly Stock Returns." *Review of Financial Studies* 30 (12): 4389–436.

Harris Poll. 2015. "The Harris Poll RQ 2015 Summary Report" (February); downloaded 4 June 2015. http://www.harrisinteractive.com/vault/2015%20RQ%20Media%20Release%20Report_020415.pdf.

Harvey, Campbell R., and Akhtar Siddique. 2000. "Conditional Skewness in Asset Pricing Tests." *Journal of Finance* 55 (3): 1263–95.

Harvey, C.R., Y. Liu, and H. Zhu. 2016. "…And the Cross-Section of Expected Returns." *Review of Financial Studies* 29 (1): 5–68.

Haugen, Robert A., and Nardin L. Baker. 1991. "The Efficient Market Inefficiency of Capitalization-Weighted Stock Portfolios." *Journal of Portfolio Management* 17 (3): 35–40.

———. 1996. Commonality in the Determinants of Expected Stock Returns." *Journal of Financial Economics* 41 (3): 401–39.

Haugen, Robert A., and A.J. Heins. 1975. "Risk and the Rate of Return on Financial Assets: Some Old Wine in New Bottles." *Journal of Financial and Quantitative Analysis* 10 (5): 775–84.

Hodgson, D.J., and Keith P. Vorkink. 2004. "Asset Pricing Theory and the Valuation of Canadian Paintings." *Canadian Journal of Economics. Revue Canadienne d'Economique* 37 (3): 629–55.

Hong, Harrison, and Marcin Kacperczyk. 2009. "The Price of Sin: The Effects of Social Norms on Markets." *Journal of Financial Economics* 93 (1): 15–36.

Hong, Harrison, and Jeremy C. Stein. 2007. "Disagreement and the Stock Market." *Journal of Economic Perspectives* 21 (2): 109–28.

Huang, Jiangwen. 2015. "A Review of Brand Valuation Method." *Journal of Service Science and Management* 8 (1): 71–76.

Huss, John, and Thomas Maloney. 2017. "Portfolio Rebalancing: Common Misconceptions." AQR working paper (February).

Ibbotson, Roger G. 2018. *SBBI Yearbook: Stocks, Bonds, Bills, and Inflation, Duff & Phelps*. Hoboken, NJ: John Wiley.

Ibbotson, Roger G., Zhiwu Chen, Daniel Y.-J. Kim, and Wendy Y. Hu. 2013. "Liquidity as an Investment Style." *Financial Analysts Journal* 69 (3): 30–44.

Ibbotson, Roger G., Jeffrey J. Diermeier, and Laurence B. Siegel. 1984. "The Demand for Capital Market Returns: A New Equilibrium Theory." *Financial Analysts Journal* 40 (1): 22–33.

Ibbotson, Roger G., and Peng Chen. 2003. "Long-Run Stock Returns: Participating in the Real Economy." *Financial Analysts Journal* 59 (1): 88–98.

Ibbotson, Roger G., and Thomas M. Idzorek. 2014. "Dimensions of Popularity." *Journal of Portfolio Management* 40 (5), Special 40th Anniversary Issue: 68–74.

Ibbotson, Roger G., and Daniel Y.-J. Kim. 2017. "Risk and Return within the Stock Market: What Works Best?" Working paper, Zebra Capital Management (30 January).

Ibbotson, Roger G., and Rex Sinquefield. 1976a. "Stocks, Bonds, Bills, and Inflation: Year-by-Year Historical Returns (1926–1974)." *Journal of Business* 49 (1): 11–47.

———. 1976b. "Stocks, Bonds, Bills, and Inflation: Simulations of the Future (1976–2000)." *Journal of Business* 49 (3): 313–38.

Idzorek, Thomas M. 2015. "How Popularity Drives Returns." *Morningstar Magazine* (April/May): 48–51.

Idzorek, Thomas M., and Roger G. Ibbotson. 2017. "Popularity and Asset Pricing." *Journal of Investing* 26 (1): 46–56.

Idzorek, Thomas M., James X. Xiong, and Roger G. Ibbotson. 2012. "The Liquidity Style of Mutual Funds." *Financial Analysts Journal* 68 (6): 38–53.

Jegadeesh, Narasimhan. 1990. "Evidence of Predictable Behavior of Security Returns." *Journal of Finance* 45 (3): 881–98.

Jegadeesh, Narasimhan, and Sheridan Titman. 1993. "Returns to Buying Winners and Selling Losers: Implications for Stock Market Efficiency." *Journal of Finance* 48 (1): 65–91.

Jensen, Michael C., Fischer Black, and Myron Scholes. 1972. "The Capital Asset Pricing Model: Some Empirical Tests." In *Studies in the Theory of Capital Markets*, edited by Michael C. Jensen. New York: Praeger.

Jensen, Michael J. 1968. "The Performance of Mutual Funds in the Period 1945–1964." *Journal of Finance* 23 (2): 389–416.

Jerison, Meyer. 1984. "Social Welfare and the Unrepresentative Representative Consumer." Working paper, SUNY Albany.

Jorion, Phillippe, and William N. Goetzmann. 1999. "Global Stock Markets in the Twentieth Century." *Journal of Finance* 54 (3): 953–80.

Kahneman, Daniel, and Amos Tversky. 1979. "Prospect Theory: An Analysis of Decision under Risk." *Econometrica* 47 (2): 263–91.

Kirman, Alan. 2006. "Heterogeneity in Economics." *Journal of Economic Interaction and Coordination* 1 (1): 89–117.

Kraus, Alan, and Robert H. Litzenberger. 1976. "Skewness Preference and the Valuation of Risk Assets." *Journal of Finance* 31 (4): 1085–100.

Kumar, Alok. 2007. "Do the Diversification Choices of Individual Investors Influence Stock Returns?" *Journal of Financial Markets* 10 (4): 362–90.

Lakonishok, Josef, Andrea Shleifer, and Robert W. Vishny. 1994. "Contrarian Investment, Extrapolation, and Risk." *Journal of Finance* 49 (5): 1541–78.

Lintner, John. 1965. "The Valuation of Risk Assets and the Selection of Risky Investments in Stock Portfolios and Capital Budgets." *Review of Economics and Statistics* 47 (1): 13–37.

———. 1969. "The Aggregation of Investor's Diverse Judgements and Preferences in Purely Competitive Security Markets." *Journal of Financial and Quantitative Analysis* 4 (4): 347–400.

Lo, Andrew W. 2017. *Adaptive Markets: Financial Evolution at the Speed of Thought*. Princeton, NJ: Princeton University Press.

Madden, Thomas J., Frank Fehle, and Susan Fournier. 2006. "Brands Matter: An Empirical Demonstration of the Creation of Shareholder Value through Branding." *Journal of the Academy of Marketing Science* 34 (2): 224–35.

Markowitz, Harry M. 1952. "Portfolio Selection." *Journal of Finance* 7 (1): 77–91.

———. 1959. *Portfolio Selection: Efficient Diversification of Investments*. New York: John Wiley.

———. 1987. *Mean–Variance Analysis in Choice and Capital Markets*. Oxford, UK: Basil Blackwell Ltd.

Mehra, Rajnish, and Edward Prescott. 1985. "The Equity Premium: A Puzzle." *Journal of Monetary Economics* 15 (2): 145–61.

———. 2003. "The Equity Premium in Retrospect." In *Handbook of the Economics of Finance*, edited by G. Constantinides, Rene M. Stultz, and M. Harris, 889–938. Amsterdam: Elsevier.

Mitton, Todd, and Keith Vorkink. 2007. "Equilibrium Underdiversification and the Preference for Skewness." *Review of Financial Studies* 20 (4): 1255–88.

Odean, Terrance. 1999. "Do Investors Trade Too Much?" *American Economic Review* 89(5): 1279–98.

Pástor, L., and R. Stambaugh. 2003. "Liquidity and Expected Return." *Journal of Political Economy* 111 (3): 642–85.

Pesando, James E. 1993. "Art as Investment: The Market for Modern Prints." *American Economic Review* 83 (5): 1075–89.

Plyakha, Yuliya, Raman Uppal, and Grigory Vilkov. 2014. "Equal or Value Weighting? Implications for Asset-Pricing Tests." Working paper (15 January). http://ssrn.com/abstract=1787045 or http://dx.doi.org/10.2139/ssrn.1787045.

Reinganum, Marc R. 1981. "Misspecification of Capital Asset Pricing: Empirical Anomalies Based on Earnings' Yield and Market Values." *Journal of Financial Economics* 9 (1): 19–46.

Rietz, Thomas A. 1988. "The Equity Risk Premium: A Solution." *Journal of Monetary Economics* 22 (1): 117–31.

Ross, Stephen A. 1976. "The Arbitrage Theory of Capital Asset Pricing." *Journal of Economic Theory* 13 (3): 341–60.

Rostad, Knut A. 2013. *The Man in the Arena: Vanguard Founder John C. Bogle and His Lifelong Battle to Serve Investors First*. New York: John Wiley.

Sharpe, William F. 1964. "Capital Asset Prices: A Theory of Market Equilibrium under Conditions of Risk." *Journal of Finance* 19 (3): 425–42.

———. 1988. "Determining a Fund's Effective Asset Mix." *Investment Management Review* (December): 59–69.

———. 1992. "Asset Allocation: Management Style and Performance Measurement." *Journal of Portfolio Management* 18 (2): 7–19.

Shefrin, Hersh, and Meir Statman. 1994. "Behavioral Capital Asset Pricing Theory." *Journal of Financial and Quantitative Analysis* 29 (3): 323–49.

Siegel, Laurence B. 2017. "The Equity Risk Premium: A Contextual Literature Review." In *Literature Reviews*. Charlottesville, VA: CFA Institute Research Foundation.

Spaenjers, Christophe, William N. Goetzmann, and Elena Mamonova. 2015. "The Economics of Aesthetics and Record Prices for Art since 1701." *Explorations in Economic History* 57 (July).

Statman, Meir. 2004. "The Diversification Puzzle." *Financial Analysts Journal* 60 (4): 44–53.

———. 2017. *Finance for Normal People: How Investors and Markets Behave*. New York: Oxford University Press.

Statman, Meir, Kenneth L. Fisher, and Deniz Anginer. 2008. "Affect in a Behavioral Asset-Pricing Model." *Financial Analysts Journal* 64 (2): 20–29.

Statman, Meir, and Denys Glushkov. 2011. "A Behavioral Asset Pricing Model with Social Responsibility Factors." Working paper (18 November).

Stattman, Dennis. 1980. "Book Values and Stock Returns." *The Chicago MBA: A Journal of Selected Papers* 4: 25–45.

Stein, John P. 1977. "The Monetary Appreciation of Paintings." *Journal of Political Economy* 85 (5): 1021–35.

Straehl, Phillip U., and Roger G. Ibbotson. 2017. "The Long-Run Drivers of Stock Returns: Total Payouts and the Real Economy." *Financial Analysts Journal* 73 (3): 32–52.

Thaler, Richard H., and Cass R. Sunstein. 2008. *Nudge: Improving Decisions about Health, Wealth, and Happiness.* New Haven, CT: Yale University Press.

Tversky, Amos, and Daniel Kahneman. 1974. "Judgement and Uncertainty: Heuristics and Biases." *Science* 185 (4147): 1124–31.

Weil, Philippe. 1989. "The Equity Premium Puzzle and the Risk-Free Rate Puzzle." *Journal of Monetary Economics* 24 (3): 401–21.

Williams, John Burr. 1938. *The Theory of Investment Value.* Cambridge, MA: Harvard University Press.

Xiong, James X., and Roger G. Ibbotson. 2015. "Momentum, Acceleration, and Reversal." *Journal of Investment Management* 13 (1): 84–95.

Xiong, James X., and Thomas M. Idzorek. Forthcoming 2019. "Quantifying the Skewness Loss of Diversification." *Journal of Investment Management* 17 (2).

Zajonc, Robert B. 1980. "Feeling and Thinking: Preferences Need No Inferences." *American Psychologist* 35 (2): 151–75.

Named Endowments

The CFA Institute Research Foundation acknowledges with sincere gratitude the generous contributions of the Named Endowment participants listed below.

Gifts of at least US$100,000 qualify donors for membership in the Named Endowment category, which recognizes in perpetuity the commitment toward unbiased, practitioner-oriented, relevant research that these firms and individuals have expressed through their generous support of the CFA Institute Research Foundation.

Senior Research Fellows

Financial Services Analyst Association

For more on upcoming CFA Institute Research Foundation publications and webcasts, please visit www.cfainstitute.org/learning/foundation.

Research Foundation monographs are online at www.cfainstitute.org.

RESEARCH FOUNDATION
CONTRIBUTION FORM

☑ **Yes**, I want the Research Foundation to continue to fund innovative research that advances the investment management profession. Please accept my tax-deductible contribution at the following level:

Thought Leadership Circle..................... US$1,000,000 or more
Named Endowment...................... US$100,000 to US$999,999
Research Fellow .... US$10,000 to US$99,999
Contributing Donor........................... US$1,000 to US$9,999
Friend .... Up to US$999

I would like to donate US$ _____.

☐ My check is enclosed (payable to the CFA Institute Research Foundation).
☐ I would like to donate appreciated securities (send me information).
☐ Please charge my donation to my credit card.
        ☐ VISA ☐ MC ☐ Amex ☐ Diners

Card Number

____ / ____   _____

Expiration Date   Name on card PLEASE PRINT
☐ Corporate Card
☐ Personal Card   _____

                  Signature

☐ This is a pledge. Please bill me for my donation of US$_____
☐ I would like recognition of my donation to be:
    ☐ Individual donation ☐ Corporate donation ☐ Different individual

_____

    PLEASE PRINT NAME OR COMPANY NAME AS YOU WOULD LIKE IT TO APPEAR

PLEASE PRINT   ☐ Mr.☐ Mrs.☐ Ms.   MEMBER NUMBER_____

_____
Last Name (Family Name)   First (Given Name)   Middle Initial

_____
Title

_____
Address

_____
City   State/Province   Country ZIP/Postal Code

Please mail this completed form with your contribution to:
The CFA Institute Research Foundation • P.O. Box 2082
Charlottesville, VA 22902-2082 USA

For more on the CFA Institute Research Foundation, please visit www.cfainstitute.org/learning/foundation/Pages/index.aspx.